LITTLE DO YOU KNOW

LITTLE DO YOU KNOW

IMAN LAVERY

NDP

NEW DEGREE PRESS

COPYRIGHT © 2021 IMAN LAVERY

LITTLE DO YOU KNOW

ISBN   978-1-63676-929-5   *Paperback*

            978-1-63676-993-6   *Kindle Ebook*

            978-1-63730-097-8   *Ebook*

For my parents

TABLE OF CONTENTS

———

AUTHOR'S NOTE

———

"Be kind. Everyone you meet is carrying a heavy burden." My fifth-grade teacher had this quote written on a big poster on her classroom wall and would frequently reference it to remind us to be mindful and kind.

These days, with curated social media accounts and our collective obsession with optimizing ourselves, it's easy to forget we all have struggles. We live in a society that demands perfection and does its best to turn us all into perfectionists.

But by calling yourself a perfectionist, you maintain a façade of perfection—of managing your burden effortlessly. At least, that's how it used to be for me. At school, I would tell my friends, "I'm such a perfectionist," but what I was really saying was I was a high achiever. I spent a lot of time on the assignment in question, and I expected to get a good grade.

I've always liked school, and I've always been good at it. I was the kid who automatically became the leader in group projects, who took advanced classes, and who got voted to be the judge during classroom mock trials. But at some point, being a good student and being *perceived* as one became inextricable, and it was impossible to tell whether I was the project leader because I could fulfill the role the best or because people assumed I could. The impression I gave—or that I was given and chose to uphold—was that I never struggled, I had no burden, or that I was carrying it with ease.

This, of course, was and is untrue. Like everyone else, I struggled with insecurity, failures, stress, the lot of it. At some point in my life, I became trapped in the cycle of being the girl who had it all together, so I hid my problems in order to live up to that reputation.

The manifestations of this cycle included small things like only telling my parents about the good grades I got. But it also kept me from auditioning to act or sing when I was younger and dreamed of being a star, fearing the embarrassment of publicly trying out and publicly failing. At the doctor's office, when my doctor asked me if I had any concerns about my body or body image, I would lie and say no, preferring to keep my insecurities to myself. In high school, after two years on the junior varsity basketball team, I quit, too afraid of the embarrassment of not making the varsity team my third year to even go to tryouts. I avoided running for positions that required a popular vote from my peers and applying for roles I wasn't already fairly confident I would get. I got boxed in by my fear of cracking the façade of having it all together.

When I started conceptualizing this book, I wanted to write about something relevant for me personally right now. Over the last few years, I've seen how this fear of failure and vulnerability plagues college students. In college, we are juggling decisions about what we want to study, what we want to do with the rest of our lives, and how we're going to get there, not to mention everything that comes with being away from home and trying to find out who we are.

We are carrying a lot. Each of us struggles to balance our unique burdens, and there is an unspoken pressure to appear as though we're managing it all just fine. It seems like everyone else is effortlessly staying on top of their courses, jobs, and multiple extracurriculars, so we feel like we always need to be doing more just to keep up.

In college, after years of unwittingly allowing my relationships and mental health to suffer, I finally started to see how pervasive this issue is, particularly among my classmates. Each of us is trying to juggle all of our commitments and worries about the future. I realized the only way I would be able to make it through college, find and pursue my passions, and create friendships to last a lifetime was by sharing my burden.

Little by little, I practiced talking to my friends when I was having a hard time and went out of my comfort zone to attend events and join student groups I was interested in. In doing so, I've built strong friendships based on trust and shared experiences, and I've discovered new interests I want to pursue. I'm by no means *cured*. Even as I've been writing this book, I've had to push myself to talk about the process with my friends and family when I'd much rather keep it to myself until I have a copy in my hand, for fear of this project not making it to publication and having to explain to them all that I failed.

It's hard to feel like you're breaking the image other people have of you by being vulnerable. I would know. But the more I've pushed myself to confide in my friends, family, and mentors, the more I've realized all of us are facing our own struggles, and we benefit from being able to talk about them with one another. We can all identify with the feeling of relief you get when you hear someone else is working through the same issue you thought you were dealing with alone.

This is something Hadley has to learn over the course of *Little Do You Know*, and it's something I'm still learning. I hope this book itself can be a first step for other college students or people who feel like they're alone in their struggles. Together, I hope to start to normalize talking about hopes, fears, and vulnerabilities and realize that trying to hold up an image of having it all together helps no one and only makes our arms tired.

I've never forgotten that poster on the wall of my fifth-grade classroom: "Be kind. Everyone you meet is carrying a heavy burden." Here's to being kind to ourselves and sharing our loads.

1

SEPTEMBER

There was a smudge on the window of the UberXL. Crushed close-up against the glass by the two duffle bags jammed in the middle seat, Hadley couldn't help but stare at it. She gave it a quick wipe with the sleeve of her sweatshirt, but it didn't budge.

Fifteen minutes had passed in silence since loading into the car at the airport. Hadley's dad was checking email in the passenger seat, and her mom was reading a book, though she seemed to be taking an inordinate amount of time on each page. Hadley couldn't even listen to anything on her headphones—her saving grace on the flight over—because they were in her backpack, which she had thrown in the trunk with the remainder of the luggage and the boxes they'd picked up from self-storage.

Nothing about this day felt like back-to-school, even though the sun was shining, and the corner of her shoe rack was digging into her side through the fabric of the duffle bag. For the first time she could remember, Hadley didn't have that familiar combination of excitement and nerves bubbling in her stomach—to see her friends, start new classes, make new memories. But she definitely didn't want to be at home, either. However she felt, she knew the only place she could figure out how to fix everything that had gone wrong was at school. She needed time to think. She needed to get back in her groove, which meant focusing on classes and focusing on the future, not the past.

"How much farther?" her mom asked no one in particular, even though it clearly said twelve minutes on the driver's GPS. She flipped her book shut.

"Another fifteen minutes. Maybe less," her dad replied, eyes still trained down at his phone.

Her mom looked down at her watch. "I can't get to the hotel too late after move-in. I need to get some sleep before the flight in the morning."

"You guys don't have to stay to unpack. I'll be fine."

Hadley's mom looked at her sharply. Her dad turned back to look at her. Hadley scrubbed at the smudge on the window.

"We're going to stay," said her dad.

"We want to see you settled in, of course," said her mom.

"Whatever works." Hadley thought the edge of the smudge was starting to come off.

"We're worried." Her mom paused, considering. "We want to make sure you're okay."

"Okay to be at school, she means," her dad cut in, "with all the stressors that can come into play."

"I'm fine," said Hadley. She felt bad for the Uber driver. He had been cracking jokes as he loaded up the car but had quickly realized the Deaton family was not in the mood and had been as silent as the rest of them during the drive.

"Of course, you're fine," said her dad. "We just want to make sure it stays that way."

Her mom nodded and reached over the duffle bags to grab her hand. She tried to hold it, but the angle and the bulk she was reaching across detracted from the intimacy she was going for, so she just gave Hadley's hand a quick squeeze and pulled her arm back to the other side of the barrier of dorm room decor and clothing.

Hadley appreciated that her parents were making an effort, she really did, but she wasn't in the mood for the barely concealed pity in their eyes when they looked at her these days. All she wanted to do was forget the events of the summer and move on. She needed a plan, and she wasn't going to be able to make one with her parents alternately babying her and keeping her at arm's length. To their credit, today, they could tell she wasn't interested in talking about it. They switched tactics to make small talk about her friends and classes and so on until the suburban homes they were driving past melted into frat houses and shops with student discount signs plastered in the windows.

The first glimpse of campus calmed Hadley down to some degree as she flashed back to the hours she'd spent studying photos of the buildings and watching day-in-the-life videos from a semipopular student YouTuber during her senior year in high school. She had already memorized the full map of the school by the time she committed, but it had never really been a question where she would go. The University of Seattle was the top liberal arts college in the Pacific Northwest. It was everything she ever dreamed of, which made it all the more frustrating that, this year, she was having trouble finding the thrill that made her fall in love with the school in the first place.

The suite was a bustle of activity when Hadley and her parents walked in, weighed down by suitcases and leftover tension from the drive to campus.

"Hadley!" Bianca dropped the box she was carrying, abandoning it partway overturned on the floor with a stack of sweaters spilling out, and rushed toward her friend, arms open wide.

"Bianca, be careful! Look at what you did," Bianca's mother admonished her, stepping around the box to greet Hadley's parents. Bianca just laughed, pulling Hadley in for a tight hug.

From around the corner, Amy appeared, her dark hair piled in a bun on top of her head and her sweatshirt sleeves pulled up to her elbows. "You're here!"

Hadley and Bianca each opened one arm to welcome her into their circle. They huddled together, a tangle of limbs, giggling and squeezing. For all her apprehension about the start of her junior year, Hadley was grateful for the uninhibited affection of her roommates and for the laughter they could pull out of her simply by their presence.

Amy's dads emerged behind her and joined Bianca's mom in exchanging pleasantries with Hadley's parents.

"Ken, Arjun, how are you?" Hadley's dad shook both of their hands.

"Still trying to get organized in here," said Ken. "It's a bit chaotic at the moment."

"Monica, I wanted to ask you. Are you guys planning to stay for a couple of days? I'd love to grab a meal or two," Bianca's mom asked as the girls finally released each other.

"We're flying back early tomorrow morning," Hadley's mom replied. "We have a bit of a quick turnaround to make."

Hadley surveyed the room. Chaotic was an understatement. Boxes and half-empty unzipped suitcases filled the floor space of the common room, nearly concealing the unassembled futon that leaned against the wall, still plastered with the logo and identification information from the storage unit Bianca had rented back in the spring. Amy's molecular modeling kit and miscellaneous lab gear were in a pile on the floor next to an assortment of posters and other wall decor. The whole mess was making Hadley's hands start to itch. Despite the hit her confidence had taken over the last month, she still knew she could organize the hell out of this room.

Bianca grinned at her, recognizing the slight squint in her friend's eyes. "So what's the plan, H? Just tell us where to move things."

The girls and their parents got to work, sorting the girls' individual belongings into their bedrooms and setting up the common room. They assembled the futon against the back wall beneath the windows at Hadley's direction, with the armchair and beanbag chair to either side, and mounted their small television on a bookshelf on the wall opposite by the door. Hadley left Bianca's artistic eye in charge of putting up posters, which she had picked out anyway.

"So tell me everything!" said Amy as she smoothed the rug over the floorboards. "I barely heard from you this summer. You must've been crazy busy."

Hadley forced a short laugh. "Yeah, just busy."

"How'd it go? Do you think you'll get a return offer?"

"I'm sure she will," Bianca chimed in, standing on the couch to stick a poster to the wall above. "She was probably the intern of the year."

Hadley gave them a small smile and excused herself from the conversation to work on her room. Her mom shot her a look as they passed each other in the hall.

Hadley organized her bedroom much as she had last year, and the year before that, with the twin XL bed tucked wall-to-wall on the smaller side of the rectangular room, leaving her with a wider square of open floor space for her school-issued desk, wardrobe, and dresser. Her mom helped her hang her string lights—a staple of any college girl's room—and her dad hung dresses and jackets on hangers. Hadley was grateful the Taylor Swift music blasting from Amy's speaker and general bustle prevented any attempt at substantive conversation with her parents. They folded and adjusted and hung in a focused silence, broken only occasionally by a "Where should I put this?" or an "It'll fit better if you do it like that." Her room didn't take long. Most of her decorations, school supplies, and general dorm necessities were in boxes waiting for her to pick them up at the mail center.

By the time things were mostly in their place, and the mess was confined to a pile of empty boxes, plastic bags, crumpled tape, and packing peanuts destined for the big trash bins by the laundry room, the sun was setting, and everyone was hungry.

"What about one last good meal?" offered Arjun. "Before you're stuck with the dining hall."

"There's that nice spot down a few blocks," said Ken. "They have good cocktails."

Hadley saw her mom glance at her watch, but neither of her parents argued. They didn't really say anything, actually, just followed the group out the door.

Hadley had to commend herself for artfully dodging the questions about her summer internship at dinner, though it didn't stop her parents from tossing sharp glances at her and each other every time it came up. She was grateful for the effusive chatter of Bianca and her mother for keeping the conversation rolling and for unwittingly masking the relative quiet from her family.

After dinner, the parents walked the girls back to their room and said their goodbyes. Hadley's mom hugged her for a long time. Her dad slipped her a couple of twenties as he embraced her. "For books. Or whatever you need," he said.

The girls closed the door behind their parents and then watched from the window as they walked to their cars and climbed into their Ubers. For all her eagerness to get away from her parents for a while, Hadley's heart nonetheless felt heavy as she watched them go, unsure whether she was sad because she would miss them, because she would rather be accompanying them home, or some combination of both.

2

――――

JUNE

The sun glowed hot in the sky like the thrill in Hadley's chest as she strode purposefully toward the Vertex headquarters. She was grateful that the weather hadn't disrupted her long-planned first-day outfit: a smart casual pairing of white jeans and a structured top she thought would strike the perfect balance between the overdressed East Coast interns and those who had already bought into the Silicon Valley t-shirt-and-jeans uniform.

To most, the sprawling, glass-walled tech haven would be daunting, but Hadley had done her research. This moment of approach was no happenstance. This was the cumulation of many years of hard work and planning just to get her foot in the door at a company with some of the most recognizable marketing in the world. Over the last few weeks, she'd spent hours poring over articles and videos about the headquarters building itself, learning everything she could about its design, history, and the day-to-day of its employees. Research gave her confidence—the best way to quell the inevitable first-day nerves—so she had scoured every corner of the internet to mine precious insights from the rare glimpses into office life released by the notoriously private company.

However, upon stepping inside, she quickly realized knowing how many months the building took to construct, the rate of employee turnover, and the company values didn't mean she knew where she was supposed to be going right now. Spotting a pair of girls approaching the front desk who were clearly too young and sharply dressed to have ever been here before, she hung back, filling the spare moment by checking her phone. Beneath a few Snapchat notifications and a headline about a miscellaneous celebrity pregnancy, there was a text from her mom: *Have an amazing first day. You're making us so proud!* followed by one too many confetti emojis. She sent back a quick and tempered red heart.

The man at the front desk gestured down a back hallway. The two girls waved in thanks as they headed in the indicated direction, so Hadley followed at a distance, straightening her posture and hoping she looked like she knew what she was doing. A handful of alternately giddy and fearful interns had entered shortly behind her. They all floated in the direction of the welcome presentation as a tentative group, and everyone sufficiently spread out so they could each pretend they knew where they were going and weren't following each other.

Upon entering the small auditorium, Hadley was pleased to find that, as planned, she had arrived after about a quarter of the name tags had already been taken. Early, but not early enough for it to be awkward. She found a seat most of the way, but not all of the way, to the front of the room. One of the girls who had come in behind her—one of the giddy types—followed her to her row.

"Do you mind?" she asked, nodding toward the seat next to Hadley.

"Not at all." Hadley politely pulled her tote bag closer on the floor in front of her. She was disconcerted to see the girl's thigh-length shift dress and denim jacket had achieved a similar smart casual effect as her own outfit.

"I'm Marianne Wallace," said the girl, extending her hand. "Software engineering."

"Hadley," said Hadley.

"So exciting, right? Being here?" Marianne didn't wait for a reply. "I've been dying to get here and meet everyone since I got my offer. The network we can build here is just unparalleled. I have a lot of ideas I want to talk to people about."

"It's exciting," Hadley agreed, shifting in her seat. She knew this type—the aspiring tech moguls. They proliferated in this region of the country. Later, she knew, against her better judgment, she would look up Marianne's LinkedIn and likely find out she was the founder of at least three startups.

"What department did you say you were in?"

"I didn't," said Hadley. "Marketing communications."

"Fun. So you study—"

"Linguistics."

Hadley watched the interest fade from Marianne's eyes. She supposed she shouldn't have been surprised to encounter someone like this. Her dad worked at a much smaller Vertex competitor, so she was no stranger to the Silicon Valley type. At the very least, Hadley understood. She could handle these people. From Marianne's perspective, a twenty-year-old linguist with marketing experience wasn't going to help her create the app that would launch her career. And Hadley herself wasn't in the market for business partners.

As they'd been talking, the seats around them had started to fill up. "Excuse me," Hadley continued, gently offering her neighbor a way out of the conversation, "I have to send a couple of emails before we get started."

With a short smile—the closed-mouth kind where you push your lips back and out against your teeth—Marianne took the out, wasting no time striking up a conversation with the guy on her other side. Thankful for the excuse to pull her phone back out, Hadley started to scroll mindlessly through Instagram, Twitter, and back again. She tried to relax the tightness that had gathered in her throat and let the looming threat of a full cohort of Mariannes slip from her mind.

Before long, the auditorium was packed with bright-eyed college undergraduates and the smell of ambition. At the front of the room, a man stood up and approached the microphone.

"Hello, interns!" The room fell silent, though the buzz in the air was no less electric. Hadley straightened in her seat. Out of the corner of her eye, she watched Marianne flip open her laptop and begin to type into a blank document. "I want to start by saying welcome to each and every one of you. My name is Matthew Sanchez. You can call me Matt. As the director of the internship program, I can tell you that you've all earned your place in this room today, so as much as we are going to make sure this summer is a transformative experience for you, we know that you all are also going to be transforming us here at Vertex."

The door at the back of the auditorium flew open with a loud thud. Every eye in the room turned to see the tall young man standing in the doorway. He looked vaguely familiar, wearing a half-untucked polo with a backpack slung over one shoulder. For a moment, Hadley couldn't place him.

"Sorry," he said, just loud enough to be heard by all. He flashed an easy smile across the room. Hadley recognized that smile. He was on Bianca's ex-boyfriend's intramural basketball team. Jacob or Jayden or something. Bianca had dragged her along to games on a handful of occasions. She was surprised she recognized him, but she supposed she couldn't blame herself if a guy with dark curls like that left an impression.

"Come on in. Find a seat," said Matt too loudly, given that there was a microphone right in front of him. Hadley looked back at the door, feeling a great deal of secondhand embarrassment, though the guy didn't seem to be feeling any firsthand embarrassment himself. "Now, where was I?" Matt continued.

The collective gaze of the interns turned back to the front of the room, but Hadley kept her head turned at a slight angle so she could glance back at the guy peripherally. He took his time, ambling down the steps to a seat on the aisle halfway down. As he sat, Hadley thought she saw a tinge of pink in his cheeks.

Following a bubbly and admittedly cliché presentation on company values—only a few steps above a scene you might find in a bad Netflix original movie—and an overview of the internship program events for the summer, the interns were finally dismissed. They filed out to the tables just outside the auditorium to collect their Vertex t-shirts and the directions to meet their supervisors. Hadley found herself corralled along with two other marketing communications interns and led to the elevators by a smiling young man in a zip-up hoodie adorned with the company logo. He pressed the up button, and the doors slid open immediately. He ushered them inside.

"Go up to five and take a right down the hall. Your team will be expecting you in the flex space," he said brightly, giving them a quick wave as the doors closed. "Good luck!"

For all her research, Hadley had no idea what a flex space was. Sounded made-up. She took a small step back as the elevator began to rise, repositioning herself so she wouldn't be the first one to step out and have to lead the others down the hall. She glanced around at the other interns. Thanks to Hadley's maneuvering, the boy was nearest to the front. He was staring intensely down at his phone. The other girl was wearing a summery dress and had a tote bag over one shoulder, looking more prepared for brunch than for a day at the office, but Hadley had to respect the look. Hadley smiled at her.

"I'm Dina," said the girl as the elevator doors opened on the fifth floor. She smiled back, looking grateful for the opening to introduce herself.

"Hadley," said Hadley.

"And I'm Nick." The boy turned briefly so as not to be left out of introductions as he took a right down the hall. Hadley and Dina followed close behind him. As it happened, Hadley needn't have worried about finding this mysterious flex space because as soon as they rounded the corner from the elevator bay, they stepped into what could truly only be described as a space.

A smattering of desks—two-sided, with a short barrier in between the two sets of computers—snaked across the floor in a sort of U shape. In the U, there were couches, beanbag chairs, and a short conference table. One wall was entirely glass, looking out over half of the parking lot and a small grassy field. The wall opposite the window was a huge white-board, covered in scribbled numbers, graphs, and bulleted lists that Hadley had no framework to understand. There was a fully decked-out coffee nook, complete with machines with an excessive number of buttons and every variety of animal-, nut-, and plant-based milk. All the desk chairs were on wheels, and Hadley watched as one woman rolled herself over to her colleague's desk and pointed at something on their computer screen.

It was an overwhelmingly collaborative space and Hadley, who was used to disappearing into the library stacks alone for hours on end to do her homework, felt a little intimidated. She tugged at her shirt, smoothing down the front. She didn't really have enough time to digest her nerves, however, because, suddenly, all of the energy in the flex space was trained on the wide-eyed trio walking in.

"You must be our new interns!" A woman in a blue dress and yellow scarf stood up from one of the beanbag chairs and walked toward them, clapping her hands together excitedly. "I'm Katie. I'll be your supervisor this summer." She shook each of their hands. "Let me introduce you to everyone!"

Hadley let herself be whirled through the space, shaking hands, learning and immediately forgetting names of twenty- and thirty-something communications managers, social media specialists, and marketing strategists. They were all effusive in their welcomes, but Hadley couldn't help but read some condescension into their smiles. Once the entire marketing communications team had gotten an up-close look at the interns, Katie showed them to their own desks. Hadley and Dina shared one table, and Nick was just a few feet away.

"My office is down the hall," said Katie, gesturing to where the flex space ended and the hallway continued across from where they'd entered. "Today we're mostly going to get you guys set up on your computers and email accounts, but normally, when you're working on projects, you can always swing by my office to ask questions or just to check-in."

Katie left them to set up their desks and follow the onboarding instructions on their new company laptops. Hadley rearranged the Vertex notebooks and Vertex pens on her desk, hung her bag on the hook under the lip of the table, and set her water bottle next to her computer. It still felt pretty corporate, but if she brought in some photos to stick on the barrier or a set of bright sticky notes, she could make this a productive workspace for herself. In fact, she would do just that. She wanted this summer to go well. And she was going to do whatever she could to make it happen.

3

On the morning of the first day of classes, Hadley's room was uncharacteristically disorganized. Her two large suitcases filled the small path between the bed and the desk, leaking stray pairs of socks and crumpled t-shirts on the floor. The packed sweaters left carelessly in a half-open dresser drawer were a far cry from the Marie Kondo folding method Bianca and Amy liked to make fun of her for. Hadley's beloved pen organizer and matching stationery set were crowded into the corner of the desktop by her two water bottles, her Starbucks tumbler, and a wide assortment of toiletries.

After snoozing her alarm three times, Hadley dragged herself out of bed and into her shower shoes.

Bianca zipped by her as she emerged from her bedroom. "Nine hours into the school year, and I'm already late for class," she said, laughing.

"Glad to know some things never change!" Amy yelled from the common room.

Normally, Hadley would have given Bianca an indulgent smile and said something along the lines of "We can't all be the responsible one." The air of confidence that had always come easy to her seemed to be buried under one of the many piles of clothes on the floor behind her. By the time she realized she should at least muster up a short laugh, Bianca was already out the door.

In the shower, Hadley let the poorly pressurized stream hit her square in the face, hoping it would pull her out of her funk, but showering wasn't quite so calming when she had to keep turning to let the narrow diameter of hot water heat her whole body. She needed to pull herself together. After everything that had happened, what she needed was a strong start to the semester, but Hadley couldn't seem to shake the shroud of gloom that tangled through all the small joys she normally found when returning to school.

Hadley dried herself off with extra fervor, scraping the now-faded towel that had been a graduation gift from her grandparents up and down her body as if she could scratch away her frustration. The anxieties that had sprung from the summer seemed to have invaded every part of her normal routine, clouding her access to her usual persona in a way she had never before experienced. She was unmoored and unsure how even to fake a sense of direction. She had so many questions about how the next semester, year, and decade of her life would look and no idea how to begin to answer them.

The one thing she had going for her today was her outfit, which she had naturally planned weeks earlier during a particularly grueling day at work—before things had entirely gone downhill. Her boss had had her sifting through endless Excel spreadsheets of e-newsletter opening rates, so Hadley self-assigned frequent breaks. Between clicking through data cells and Google Chrome search tabs on how to work

Microsoft Excel—a program in which she had confidently assured the hiring manager she was well-versed—she had surfed online shopping websites for the late summer sundress and jacket pairing.

From her bedroom window, as she got ready, Hadley could see the first-day bustle and feel the energy exuding from the street below. People were hugging and laughing, catching up with friends they probably hadn't spoken to since the previous spring and making empty promises to grab lunch sometime soon. The sun ignited the scene, reflecting the brilliance of the students' big smiles, tanned skin, and shiny new entries on their LinkedIn pages. Hadley closed her eyes and focused her attention on her chest as if she could absorb and embody the excitement in the air by sheer force of will.

"Are you going to the south end of campus?" Amy poked her head into the room, disrupting Hadley's attempt at reverie.

"Yes," she replied, crouching to rummage through the duffle bag full of shoes in the corner. "Give me a minute."

"No rush. We can grab breakfast on the way." Amy paused as she moved to shut the door behind her, flashing Hadley a smile. "You look great, by the way. You're always so put together. I can't even be bothered for the first day back." She gestured toward her t-shirt and denim shorts.

Hadley laughed by way of response because she didn't know how else to answer. She didn't feel put together. But at least everyone else would still see her that way. She slipped on her boots, adjusted her tote bag on her shoulder, smoothed a stray lock of hair, and took a deep breath.

Amy was waiting for her by the door, backpack slung over one shoulder. "Our first day of the second half of college. Are you ready for this?"

No, Hadley thought. "Of course," she said.

Stepping out into the bright sunshine did not help assuage Hadley's nerves. On the contrary, looking out over the sea of students crisscrossing the lawn, she was suddenly seized by the fear she might run into Jayden. That was the last thing she needed today. It had been a few weeks since he'd last tried to reach out, which was fair enough considering she'd been ignoring him for weeks before that. She still remembered his last text: *Seems like I need to give you space. Hope you're good.* Ideally, she would be able to avoid him for the rest of the year, but one day at a time. Hadley kept her eyes trained at the ground in front of her. If she avoided eye contact with everyone, then she wasn't actually seeing anyone.

Amy, chattering away about some scheduling drama to do with setting up an anthropology independent study course with her favorite professor, was thankfully too absorbed in all the excitement to notice her roommate's downward gaze.

"Starbucks?" Amy asked, pausing in the middle of her recitation of the email she'd sent the registrar. She pointed across the quad toward the popular on-campus location, ever-full of students.

That popularity made Hadley pause. She thought she could probably use a venti cold brew to get her through the day, but taking this detour meant traversing the packed quad and spending long minutes loitering around one of the most densely packed places to be on any given morning during the school year. Hadley just wanted to make it to her classroom with her sanity intact.

"I'm not actually that hungry," she said. Better not to risk it. "You go. I need to get to class."

Amy looked down at her phone and then shot Hadley a strange look that might've had to do with the fact classes didn't start for another twelve minutes. But Amy knew Hadley and would probably just assume she wanted to be early to meet the professor and get a good seat.

As Hadley had hoped, her roommate just shrugged. "Suit yourself," she said. "If you ask me, today calls for a Frappuccino and a breakfast sandwich."

Hadley smiled and waved goodbye as their paths diverged. As soon as Amy turned away, she picked up her pace, holding her phone in front of her face like a shield from awkward reunions with acquaintances and any potential sightings of one very particular boy. She arrived at the lecture hall for her history course on the Cold War unscathed and found a spot on the aisle near the back—not in the middle toward the front where she normally sat—and quickly set up her laptop on the fold-out desk.

After an hour of note-taking about mutually assured destruction, Hadley slipped back across campus to her dorm, stopping by the nearby mini-mart to pick up some basic supplies for emergency meals in the room. She didn't even bother trying to meet up with her roommates for lunch, opting instead to throw together peanut butter and jelly on a paper towel on their common room coffee table and eat it alone while she watched an old episode of *Grey's Anatomy*.

Thanks to her careful planning of routes and quick pace, she made it through her internet linguistics seminar and morphology lecture without incident. She felt a wave of relief flood her as she stepped into her suite at the end of the day, her backpack full of syllabi. Bianca was sprawled out on the couch, scrolling on her phone.

She looked up. "How was your first day?"

"Long," said Hadley.

"You're telling me. I had three classes back-to-back. No lunch for me on Mondays, I guess. I've been on my phone for the last half hour looking at the same ten Instagram posts over and over."

Hadley discarded her bag on the floor and squeezed in next to Bianca. "Can we watch a movie?"

"That's the best idea I've heard all day." Bianca craned her neck to look around the corner and down the hallway, as if it were at all possible to see into any of the rooms from that angle. "Amy! Get in here!" She turned back to Hadley. "We're getting takeout. I know we're supposed to be responsible about food costs, but I could kill for some fried rice and a rom-com."

"Takeout?" Amy called from her room. "I love you. I'm going to change into sweats."

"And that's the best idea *I've* heard all day," said Hadley.

"I have a discount code for Uber Eats," said Bianca. "Add whatever you want." She handed Hadley her phone.

Hadley added enough honey walnut prawns, moo shu pork, and gyoza to the cart to last her for the next few days. Her stomach was already growling at the thought of some comfort food, and it wouldn't hurt to stock up on snacks in the room if she ever needed to avoid the crowded dining halls.

Bianca slumped into the corner of the couch as Hadley gave her back her phone. "Why do I feel like this semester is going to be so exhausting?" she said.

"I'm already exhausted," said Amy, ambling in wearing sweatpants and an oversized University of Seattle sweatshirt.

Hadley could feel herself start to relax. She kind of hated herself for thinking it, but it made her feel better that her roommates hadn't loved their first day back either. But as Amy settled in beside her to wait for the food to arrive, she knew she couldn't let this feeling last. She couldn't go through the entire year tiptoeing around campus and only eating in her room. She could at least admit that much to herself. She needed things to go back to how they were the year before. She needed to start acting like herself again. Something needed to be done.

4

By the beginning of her second week at the office, Hadley had grown wary of lunchtime. There were a number of problems that arose in and around that midday hour, not the least of which being that all the interns seemed eager to cut it short. On that first day, Hadley had stayed close to Dina and Nick. The marketing communications trio had found a roost out on the lawn with a few product design and business development interns.

Not even thirty minutes in, however, people began to disappear, citing a desire to track down an executive to get industry pointers, intimating the existence of some important project they simply could not put off another minute, or simply claiming to want to get back to work. As far as Hadley could tell, it had started when one of the business development guys said he wanted to see if he could get an informational interview with the COO. Everyone else was suddenly stumbling over each other to come up with some equally lofty reason they could not waste any more time at lunch.

Within a few days, some interns were taking lunch late in the afternoon or even popping into the cafeteria to grab something to eat back at their desks. Hadley felt like she was still at school, surrounded by people constantly rushing off to some important commitment, except at school, she was normally one of those people. She couldn't tell whether she was missing something important or whether she just hadn't yet found her stride. Either way, the feeling of being behind nagged in the back of her mind.

Even the cafeteria itself was anxiety-inducing. Despite the rows and rows of food options, there was always a disproportionate amount of people in line for the salad bar, mechanically tossing kale and quinoa into their bowls. Hadley wondered at the automation of the whole thing, watching as people strode into the cafeteria, cell phones brandished in front of their faces, and walked straight over to pick up a mixing bowl and join the line. Perhaps it was the safety of having a routine, knowing where to go and what to do. Or perhaps it was the inherent pressure to posture at healthy living that came with being in this part of California. Either way, Hadley couldn't judge because she too found herself drifting toward the salad bar each day around noon, more comfortable joining the crowd than wandering around to peruse the options and risk giving off the impression that she didn't know what she was doing.

Today, Hadley walked into the cafeteria alone. She had made the mistake of closing her laptop and standing up before asking Dina if she wanted to go to lunch so that when her desk mate had waved her ahead, saying she wanted to finish what she was working on, it was too late to pretend she didn't actually want to go yet either. Nick, her second option for companionship, was nowhere to be found. Now,

Hadley was vacillating at the entrance to the cafeteria, slowing her movements in hopes she would spot a group of people she could sit with before she ended up looking lost, holding her tray in the middle of the room like a new student in a high school movie. She was gearing herself up to move toward the food lines alone when she heard someone come up behind her.

"You go to the University of Seattle." She turned to find the boy who was late on the first day—the one she recognized from school—looking at her with a lopsided grin. He was taller than she had imagined from afar, with the kind of dark curly hair that looked better the more disheveled it got—the kind that made Hadley frustrated about the amount of time and number of products it took to tame her own.

She gave him a tentative smile. "I do. You do too, right?"

He nodded. "I'm Jayden."

"Hadley Deaton," said Hadley. "I mean, just Hadley." She blushed.

Jayden grinned and gestured toward the food displays. "What are you after? The possibilities are endless." He strode toward the hamburger counter, and Hadley kept up behind him, eager not to lose a friendly face and mealtime companion.

"I usually just go for a salad," she said quietly. She thought he wouldn't hear her over the cafeteria bustle as he intently perused the meal options, but he threw her a look of utter confusion. Hadley cringed. Frequenting the salad bar was primarily a product of the ease of the process and the comfort of the long lines—knowing everyone else was making the same choice—but she didn't quite know how to explain that sentiment aloud.

"Not today," said Jayden. "We have to take advantage of the free lunch while we can. Have you even seen all the things they have here?"

Hadley had to admit she hadn't, having thus far preferred to head straight to the counter she could trust rather than aimlessly wandering through the other options and risk losing Dina and Nick in the throng.

Jayden led her to each table—the picture of ease, seemingly unaware of the fast-paced lunchtime habits of the rest of the room. He showed her where the Indian food counter was and the acai bowl bar, and there was even a sushi table tucked way in the back, with a smaller line of people waiting, that hadn't caught her eye before, focused as she was on the salad cohort.

Nearly twenty minutes had passed before the pair emerged onto the lawn—Hadley with a plate of sushi and a side of fries and Jayden with a cheeseburger and a slice of pizza. Hadley had arrived down at the cafeteria almost exactly at noon, but already she could see some of the other interns dropping their trays on the dirty dishes conveyer belt or scampering back toward the elevators with their salads.

The lawn was an expanse in every sense of the word. It stretched out from the back side of the headquarters for nearly a quarter-mile, a carefully designed landscape that included an outdoor pavilion, smatterings of picnic tables, two abstract metal sculptures, and a full adult-size playground structure for *stress relief*. Near the center of the lawn, there was a dry fountain—the kind where streams of water shoot up straight out of the ground—that could be lit up in different colors for holidays and special company events. Hadley had never taken much time to look at the space and all that it held, always too focused on finding an appropriate group of people to sit with or skipping going outside altogether.

Jayden and Hadley set their trays down on one of the outdoor tables on the far side of the seating area, an umbrella angled to protect them from the hot summer sun. Without the urge to excuse herself from the table as soon as possible or the frenetic energy of sitting with a dozen eager interns, Hadley actually found sitting outside quite peaceful. People sat in small groups, scattered across the tables and on the grass. She and Jayden were off to one side, able to look out over the entire scene, watching people laugh, chat, eat, and check their phones from afar.

"How was your first week?" Hadley asked once they sat down, grasping for an appropriate conversation starter.

Jayden chewed a bite of pizza and swallowed. "The work's alright. I'm in software engineering, so it's pretty much what I was expecting. It's the people that are strange."

"In what way?" Hadley asked, even though she thought she knew. She pictured Marianne Wallace's condescending smile.

"It's just a different vibe from Chicago, or even from Seattle. People at school aren't this into themselves."

Hadley let out a startled laugh. "Tell me about it. I grew up here."

Jayden laughed, but he looked at her thoughtfully. "Doesn't sound easy."

"It was fine." She smiled, hoping, for a reason elusive even to herself, to assure him of her having had an idyllic childhood in Silicon Valley, free from the pressures and concerns of life in social-media-era California. She wanted to change the subject. "So what year are you at school?"

"Senior," Jayden said. "I guess this is the summer to try and secure a return offer, but I don't know if this is the place for me. You?"

"I'll be a junior. I thought—well, I think I might come back here. I don't think there's a better place to be for marketing. Vertex isn't the kind of place you turn down, you know? If I do get an offer."

"You can always turn it down if it's not where you want to be." Jayden looked over at her.

"It is where I want to be, though." Hadley felt herself getting flustered. "I mean, I've been working toward an internship here for years. It speaks highly of all of us that we're here right now."

"Of course," Jayden raised his hands in concession, "we've all worked hard. But just because we worked hard to be here doesn't mean we need to stay."

"Then what does it mean?" Hadley's agitation was turning to frustration, but she did her best to hide it. She didn't know what Jayden was trying to get at or whether he was trying to call her out for something, but she didn't like the feeling either way.

"I'm just saying I think it's okay to make the most of this summer—enjoy it and learn from it and stock up on free t-shirts—and then decide that it's not for me. It doesn't mean I'm taking it for granted, just that I'm being aware of what I want and don't want. Anyways, I'm not saying that's how I feel, just that I'm not sure yet."

While Hadley could feel her face getting warm—unsure whether Jayden's comment was pointed or just introspective—he seemed completely calm. He was leaning back in his chair. His legs stretched out in front of him. He wasn't even looking at her as he spoke, his eyes following the movement across the outdoor dining area. He seemed entirely content to sit back, enjoying his free Vertex catering, and disparage the people who worked here. Hadley wasn't thinking about the fact she, too, had been put off by the fast-paced salad-eating tendencies of her colleagues half an hour earlier. She was only thinking about the fact her plan, the plan she'd been crafting in her mind for years, was to secure the very return offer he was scorning and move back down to California after graduation. She resented his ability to put so little stake in this summer when this summer and this internship meant everything to her and her future.

"I forgot," said Hadley. Jayden looked over at her, his arms crossed lazily over his chest. "I forgot I have a project I'm supposed to submit." She stood up, gathering the refuse of her meal onto her tray. "I have to run."

Jayden nodded. "I'll see you around, HD."

She gave him a look, taking a moment to recognize her own initials. No one had ever called her HD before. She was always just Hadley. She said goodbye and strode away quickly. She needed time to think about this, to process this interaction with this boy. She wasn't sure she liked him. But she had to think about it.

As she passed back through the cafeteria, pausing to drop her tray onto the conveyor belt, she glanced over at the salad bar. The line was nearly as long as it had been when she first arrived. She almost didn't see Dina rush from the end of the bar back out toward the elevators, salad in one hand, cell phone in the other. Hadley slowed her pace and ambled toward the stairs, tucked behind a door down around the corner from the elevators, suddenly far less eager to return to her desk.

5

SEPTEMBER

Hadley hadn't had high expectations for the decor of the campus mental health clinic. Still, she had expected there to at least have been some semblance of an effort to disguise the grossly underfunded reality of the program. The reception area carpet and the upholstery of the waiting room armchairs were a similar mottled shade of purple-gray, presumably to circumvent the visibility of accidental stains through the choice of a fabric that looked stained in its natural state. Clunky desktop computers with thick-keyed keyboards protected the receptionists from the mysterious ailments of the students who wandered out of the elevator—a painfully laughable comparison to the sleek new Mac models that peppered the school's tourist-accessible libraries and laboratories. There was little in the way of decoration, aside from a few roughly framed photos of the campus that could have been—and perhaps were—purchased at the gift shop next to the admissions office.

Hadley smoothed the front of her shirt and tucked a stray strand of hair behind her ear as she approached the check-in desk. As little as she wanted to be here right now, the best thing she could do was put her best face forward, try to be helpful, and hope sitting through a session or two would quell her parents' concerns.

The receptionist looked to be in her early thirties, with long acrylic nails and voluminous curly hair that was barely held back by a thick red headband. She was not-so-surreptitiously scrolling on her phone, which was propped on the desk against a pad of sticky notes. On the elevated front edge of the desk, between a stack of pamphlets detailing the warning signs of depression and a half-full pen holder, there was a smiling lucky cat figurine, the kind that actually waved when you flicked the arm. Though its placement was clearly an attempt to put patients at ease, she found its smile and location disconcerting, like it was there to wish her a twisted sort of luck in her appointment.

"How can I help you, hon?"

Hadley looked up from the smirking cat. The receptionist was looking at her with a half-hearted smile—lips together, no teeth, like she'd been working here long enough that she had co-opted the disinterested neutrality of the office.

"I have an appointment with Dr. Rowe," she replied and was surprised to find herself speaking scarcely above a whisper, even though the waiting room was empty save for one guy in the corner who was nodding along to something playing on his headphones.

The receptionist asked for her name and spent a few moments typing, the thick keys clicking loudly with each tap. "Is this your first visit?" She didn't wait for an answer. "Here are a couple of questionnaires you'll need to complete. Fill them out as best as you can, and Dr. Rowe will come out to grab you in a few minutes." She gestured toward the pen holder.

Hadley selected one of the identical pens branded with the school logo at random, careful not to nudge the arm of the lucky cat as she pulled it out. She selected a chair at the opposite end of the row from the boy in the corner and perched herself on the edge of the seat. The first page of the packet was straightforward, asking about her medical history and whether she was taking any medications. *No.*

The second sheet was titled *Alcohol and Drug Use History*. She answered truthfully about her weekend drinking habits and that no one had ever told her she had a problem with alcohol. The fourth question down asked, *Has your use of alcohol ever caused a relationship problem with anyone?* Involuntarily, memories of a few fumbling drunken hookups flashed through her head. She hesitated—but only briefly—and checked the *no* box.

The third section of the questionnaire was daunting—106 yes or no questions. Most of them, like *Do you believe you're not as good, as smart, or as attractive as most other people?* or *Do you often feel people are threatening or insulting you by the things they say or do?* were a quick *no*, but for a handful of them, she hesitatingly checked *yes.*

Do you find it hard to be 'open' even with people you are close to? Hadley flashed back to the summer, to meeting Jayden, to letting him get to know her, to where it all went south. She pulled herself away from the memories. If anything, he was the proof the closer she got to someone, the harder it became for her to open up. *Yes.*

Are you afraid to do things that might be challenging or to try anything new? This one was hard. She wavered. Her pen floated over both options before marking a hesitant check in the blank space between the *yes* and *no* boxes.

When she got to *Do you think a lot about the perfect romance that will be yours someday?* she checked *no* a little too fast.

The last section was *Current Life Situations.* When asked to rate the severity of her problems on a scale from one to ten, she selected a three for mildly upsetting. If she'd been asked in the moment, over the summer, it would have been an easy ten, but now, the most upsetting part of it all was the memory of it. In answer to *When did your problems begin?* she wrote simply, *the summer.* Hadley was considering how to describe her attitude and behavior at school under the *Current School Life* subsection when she heard her name called. She looked up.

Dr. Rowe was younger than Hadley expected—probably not much older than the receptionist—and had bright red hair that fell to her shoulders. She wore a teal top tucked into a pair of white dress pants and had an eclectic stack of colorful bracelets on each wrist. She smiled warmly at Hadley as she stood up, gathering her backpack and the questionnaire into her arms.

"I'm Angie. It's wonderful to meet you." Dr. Rowe—Angie—reached out to shake Hadley's hand. "I can take the paperwork from you. Come right this way. My office is just around the corner."

She gestured for Hadley to walk into the office first. The room, while small, was a warm reprieve from the dismal reception area. A small, pale blue chaise longue and gray armchair occupied most of the floor space, each decorated with bright yellow patterned throw pillows. The wooden desk was tucked into one corner, laden with notepads, assorted trinkets, and two potted succulents. Sunlight streamed through the large window, and Hadley couldn't help but feel she had stepped into a world completely other than the one with the stained carpeting and palpable disinterest.

"Go ahead and take a seat wherever you like."

Hadley sat tentatively on one end of the chaise longue, unsure whether she was supposed to put her feet up or lie down as they did in the movies. Angie sat down in the gray armchair opposite her, skimming through the pages of the questionnaire. Having flipped through each page briefly, she looked up at Hadley and smiled.

"So, Hadley, why don't we start with the basics? What brings you here today?"

Hadley had been expecting some form of this question, having Googled "what questions does a therapist ask first session" the night before, but she still struggled to put it in words. She did want to be honest—to show she was capable of working through her problems and figuring out the next steps herself.

"I think my parents were hoping you could help me talk through some things. I had a bit of a rough summer, but I'm fine now. I'm ready to move on, but my parents are still worried about me, I guess."

"Would you like to tell me a little bit about what happened?"

Hadley pinched the hem of her skirt between two fingers. It was a cute one—houndstooth, and slightly formfitting. She'd chosen it because she wanted to look put together, as if she needed to prove her case, prove she really was fine. But she didn't actually need to prove anything, did she? She could decide what she did and didn't want to say.

"Not particularly. I'm not sure if that's really going to help. I had a hard time this summer. Things didn't go as I'd hoped with my internship, and there was one day where it all came to a head, but, well, I'm fine now. I honestly just need to get things back on track and move forward."

"I see." Angie looked at her thoughtfully and jotted something down on her notepad. That look reminded her of Jayden, the way he looked at her over the summer—penetrating, like he genuinely wanted to understand what was going on in her mind. "And what do you mean by back on track?"

Hadley's back was to the window, so the sunlight illuminated Angie's face, making her red hair look like it was on fire. She thought for a moment.

"Well, not back on track, exactly. I guess I need a new track."

"A new track." Angie flipped back through Hadley's questionnaire. As she did, each page caught the light at just the right angle so that the typed questions and pen check marks were lost in the glare, so that for a moment, they each looked completely blank. Hadley half-wished they really were blank—that she hadn't been quite so honest filling out those pages.

"I noticed here on question twenty-three, where it asks whether you're afraid to do new or challenging things, you marked somewhere between yes and no. Can you elaborate on that choice?"

Hadley took a deep breath. Perhaps giving Angie something—just a little bit of her true feelings—would appease her enough she could satisfy whatever required introspection her parents wanted her to do.

"I don't think it's really new things or challenging things that are a problem, necessarily. I guess it's more risky things that are stressful. But that seems normal, right?"

"Of course, I think most people are risk-averse, but when you say risky, in what way do you mean?" Angie's pen was poised over her notes.

Hadley felt herself starting to get a little flustered. She sat up even straighter on the edge of the couch. The note-taking part was stressing her out, making her feel like she was saying something wrong. She didn't know quite how to put her thoughts into words. Challenge at school was fine, in her classes and assignments and things like that. On the other hand, she hated the idea of running for a leadership position in a club or, more accurately, running for a position she didn't already have a pretty good idea she would win. She didn't like new things that involved applications or interviews, but, really, who did like putting effort into an endeavor only to fail?

"You know, where things can go wrong. Like when you put yourself out there, and then people see when you mess up. I guess I avoid that. I've always hated the idea of tryouts, for example. Because it's so public, but that's why I like to have a plan and time to prepare. Really, what I need is to figure out what I actually want to do with school and my career and stuff and then I can work toward it as I did before."

Angie tapped her pen absentmindedly on her chin. "It sounds to me like you like certainty. Does that sound right?"

Hadley nodded.

"Well, once you figure out what your new track is going to be, do you think you are going to worry it will lead you to the same situation as whatever happened this summer all over again?"

"I'm already worried about that," Hadley admitted.

Angie gave her a look so full of empathy and kindness that it was almost disconcerting, especially with her hair like flames framing her smiling eyes. "Then maybe having a direction isn't the real problem here."

Hadley felt the heat rise in her cheeks. She didn't know quite why she felt embarrassed, but Angie's penetrating stare burrowed into her, as if she was seeing into her very soul, seeing that Hadley didn't want to be here, that she didn't really think she needed to be here. And then she felt her hands get clammy, realizing, like it or not, her new therapist wasn't going to let her work through her summer problems on her own.

6

JULY

Hadley's keys clinked against the glass as she pushed open the imposing main doors at the entrance of Vertex. She had yet to get used to the torturous blast of the air conditioning throughout the building and had made the mistake of leaving her sweater in her car. Ambling down the path toward the parking lot, however, she couldn't help but recall a dinner conversation she'd had with her parents a few nights earlier and wonder whether forgetting her sweater wasn't quite as innocent a mistake as it seemed.

"How much are you loving Vertex?" her mom had asked between mouthfuls of grilled asparagus. They had been sitting in the backyard under the shade of the umbrella, working their way through a haul of farmer's market produce hot off the grill.

"So much," Hadley immediately replied.

And that was it. The conversation moved on. Her mom launched into a saga about a copyright issue she'd run into while crafting a campaign for one of her clients at the advertising agency, and her dad worked his way through his second beer. But Hadley's mind was stuck on her mom's question. She'd replied automatically, the way she—like everyone else—said "fine" when someone asked how she was doing, even if she was not fine. She hadn't really stopped to think about her answer.

How much *was* she loving Vertex? She was, of course, enduringly grateful to be there, and the internship program was so highly renowned. There was no doubt she was having a truly valuable learning experience. But she could not quiet the nagging voice in the back of her mind that wouldn't stop complaining about the endless spreadsheets of consumer demographic data and the overwrought process of turning the numbers into visually appealing charts and graphs. It was—she scarcely dared articulate it even to herself—kind of boring her.

And, of course, this all led back to the sweater she'd left in the passenger seat. Perhaps some part of her mind had told her to leave the sweater on purpose so she would have a reason to escape the frenetic energy of the flex space, even for only a few minutes.

Hadley felt a surge of frustration toward Jayden and what he'd said about Vertex—surely he'd gotten into her head and planted these doubts. Besides, of course, the work assigned to the interns was going to be boring. She just needed to work her way up as everyone else did, and she would find the light of excitement she always saw in her mom's eyes when she was talking about a new campaign idea. Her dad, too, could never stop talking about the latest news in the tech world. She would get there. She just needed to have a little faith.

It made her nervous, this brief moment of doubt. After everything—the years of building her resume, the months of going through the recruiting process, the weeks of preparing to start her internship—Hadley couldn't afford a tremor in her resolve. She was lucky. Most of her friends were only just figuring out what career paths they wanted to pursue. But she'd always been one to plan. She needed to have direction, a goal. That was how she did her best work.

Hadley clicked the unlock button, and her car flashed its headlights at her—quelling, for the moment, her overactive mind. She pulled open the passenger side door and yanked the abandoned sweater off the seat. All this over a sweater. And it was probably all in her head. Nonetheless, Hadley quickened her pace, and she walked back toward the building as if to prove to herself she wanted to get back to work.

Inside, Hadley turned down the hall toward the staircase by the cafeteria. She had gotten into the habit of taking the stairs to and from lunch whenever she was alone, attracted by the quiet and by the repetition of each step, up or down. She found it calming. Or maybe she just liked having a longer commute back up to her desk.

Distracted by the echo of her mom's voice in her mind asking her how much she was loving Vertex, she didn't register surprise at there being another person walking toward the door to the stairwell, and she didn't register it was Jayden until he was holding the door open for her.

"HD," he said by way of greeting. He was giving her a look, a kind of half-smirk. She felt herself flush just a little bit. She knew what that smirk was saying. Hadley had been avoiding him.

Ever since their contentious conversation on the lawn— not exactly a brawl, but every time Hadley thought about it, it became more and more tense in her memory—she'd avoided being in a situation where they said more than "hello" to each other or gave a nod of recognition. She'd doubled down on the quick lunch strategy of the other interns, though she had been branching out with her meal choices. It wasn't that she particularly disliked him or anything, but she hadn't figured him out, and that was frustrating. He seemed like someone who could quickly become a distraction, so different from the kind of person who worked at Vertex—the kind of person she was trying to become.

"Thanks," said Hadley, slipping through the open door and into the stairwell. She began to climb the steps, feeling Jayden's presence behind her. She waited for him to say something, to start a conversation. They climbed the first flight in silence, save for the sound of their shoes colliding with the metal steps. At the top, Hadley decided she had to say something. She slowed her pace, waiting for him to come into stride next to her.

"So you found the stairs, too."

"More like I sought them out," he replied. "I get restless sitting at my desk."

Hadley nodded. "So, how's it going? Work, I mean."

"Not too bad." She glanced up to see he was looking down at her. He looked thoughtful. "Actually, not great."

Hadley was taken aback by his confession. "Why's that?" They were at the top of the second flight now, but they both began to slow their pace.

"Feeling a little trapped by this whole work routine. You know: wakeup, nine-to-five, eat, sleep, repeat. Half the reason I applied for this job was to come to California, and I haven't really been able to do much. No car makes it hard."

"I have a car," said Hadley without thinking. She blushed and looked down at her feet as they climbed the next step. Why did she say that? She did have a car, of course, but was he going to think she wanted to hang out? What if he said no?

Jayden squinted at her, scrutinizing. "You live close by?"

"Yeah. Like twenty minutes from here."

"So what do you recommend, then?" He gestured around as if the entire city was visible from this claustrophobic little stairwell. Hadley hoped she wasn't turning red. He didn't mention what she said about having a car at all. He was trying to play it off, to let her down easy. She shouldn't have mentioned it. Now she was really going to have to avoid him. She might even have to go back to the salad bar. At least there she could be sure she would never run into him in the line.

"Being near the water is nice." She cringed. *The water is nice?* That was all she could say? "You can find some smaller beaches that are less touristy," she added quickly.

Jayden nodded. "I definitely need to get to the beach."

"Lots of great food, obviously. Some really cool places for ice cream." Hadley couldn't stop talking. She needed to fill the space, to leave no air left for her embarrassment. "There's also a movie theater nearby. One of the ones where you can order a meal from your seat, and they'll bring it to you. And some cool museums."

She looked up at him. He was grinning. Was he laughing at her? He must think she was crazy—going on and on like this. She stopped talking abruptly.

They were almost to the fifth floor. Hadley had sped up her pace again when she realized the conversation was going south. She practically leaped up the last few steps.

"So was that an offer?" Jayden asked.

Hadley spun around. "Was what an offer?"

"Before. When you said you have a car. Was that an offer?" He was leaning on the railing of the landing, that half-smirk back on his face.

"Oh," said Hadley. "I—yes, yeah, sure. I guess."

"Cool. You can show me one of those beaches you were talking about."

"Yeah," said Hadley. "Sure."

Jayden pulled out his phone, opened up a new contact, and offered it to her. She mistyped her phone number twice before she got it right.

"Cool," said Jayden. "Yeah, cool. I'll text you then." His tone was confident, but as he said "then," his pitch turned up—ever so slightly—making it sound like he was asking a question.

"Sure," said Hadley. She turned back around and slipped through the door onto the fifth floor. As the door swung shut behind her, she realized she probably should have said goodbye, but it was too late.

She ambled down the hall, torn between trying to process and trying to get her head back into working mode. Entering the flex space—so wide open, so opposite from the stairwell—felt strange, even though she'd only been gone for ten minutes. She smiled at Dina, who was typing furiously with an empty salad container next to her computer, and settled into her seat. She opened her latest spreadsheet, but something was nagging at her, distracting her.

"Not great," Jayden had said. After just one conversation at lunch, he had been honest with her. Hadley knew she would have said "fine" if he had asked her how she was doing, even if she was not fine. Actually, especially if she was not fine. She still didn't get Jayden. She considered herself to be a perceptive person, but she couldn't quite figure him out. What she did know, however, was it felt good to be trusted with his honest assessment of "how he was doing." Even if she couldn't read him, at least it seemed he saw something trustworthy in her.

7

OCTOBER

After two more sessions with Angie, Hadley wasn't feeling any more enlightened or less burdened than she had been when she first got back to campus. Mostly, she felt like all the worrying over what she might be asked to talk about was just exacerbating her anxiety. It was hard enough trying to stay on top of her course load and extracurriculars while all the time scrambling to figure out what she wanted to do with the rest of her life.

Angie was nice—she wasn't denying that—and far less intimidating than she had expected. She sort of reminded Hadley of a cool aunt, in a different context, of course, but sitting across from Angie in an office for an hour while she tried to get Hadley to relive her worst day didn't exactly generate a warmth of feeling.

In yesterday's session, Angie had asked her about her roommates. "Tell me about them," she'd said. "What are they like? What do they mean to you?" Hadley felt herself tuning out even as she opened her mouth to respond, letting a string of compliments and the story of how she'd first met Bianca and Amy slip from her lips while she thought about the two essays due in the next three days she hadn't yet started.

She couldn't quit, of course, primarily because her parents absolutely would not let her, but also because she didn't want to let Angie down. So she answered all of the questions about seemingly random aspects of her life and relationships, hoping to strike the right balance of cheerful confidence and thoughtful introspection. Maybe if she could both demonstrate her ability to talk openly about her life and stay on top of her work, all while telling Angie she had found her new calling once she figured out what exactly that was, then she might not have to keep going to therapy. If she could just get a grip on herself, Angie would have to believe she was making progress in their sessions.

But first, she had to work on her essays.

Hadley stepped into the main library, tote bag weighing down her shoulder with books and notebooks and her laptop. This was Hadley's favorite place to buckle down and work. She could almost feel her posture straighten and her resolve strengthen as she walked through the doors, the familiar entryway priming her for a day of focus. These days she felt like she didn't know all that much about anything, but she at least knew how to churn out an essay in one day. It was an art she had perfected after many years of putting too much on her own plate and having to crank out school assignments shortly before the deadline. If she could finish an entire essay today—and she knew she could—then she would have plenty of time in the next two days to work on the second one. She ran through the numbers in her head. She could easily write at least a page an hour, so she could work for a couple of hours, pop over to the cafe to grab something to eat, and then finish the paper by dinnertime.

She walked into the main hall of the library—the room featured in every brochure and admissions presentation. The ceilings were breathtakingly high, and the hall spanned the entire length of the building so that it looked just about endless. Rows of long wooden tables lined each side of the center pathway, and bookshelves and arched windows lined the walls. This room was part of the reason she had fallen in love with the campus in the first place. Hadley had been able to picture herself here, hunched over one of the tables, surrounded by impressive-looking books and impressive people typing, note-taking, and scribbling in notebooks. Now, this was a space that gave her back some measure of her confidence, knowing she had arrived with a task she could complete if she sat down and put her mind to it.

She found a spot at one of the emptier tables, with only one other person sitting at the opposite end, and set up her workspace. This was an important part of her routine—pulling everything out of her bag and arranging it in its particular spot, laid out in a halo around her to maximize her access to everything she needed. First, Hadley slipped her laptop out of its case and opened it in front of her, then untangled her charging cord and plugged it into the outlet under the table. She pulled out her notebook and flipped it open to the page where she'd sketched out a quick outline of her paper and placed it to the right of her laptop. Her planner went just behind and to the left of her laptop, where she could just glance over at her to-do list to keep herself focused on what she needed to get done. She had written out each step of the process of writing her paper with breaks included so she could check off each step and give herself that small rush of accomplishment as she saw the list of checkmarks grow. The books she was using for reference and evidence went to her left, and, finally, she put a pencil next to her notebook in case she needed to jot down any thoughts so she wouldn't lose them as she was writing.

This she could do. She looked over at her to-do list. *Number one: format document.* Easy. She adjusted her font, typed out her header, and formatted the page numbers. Then she picked up her pencil and checked the box on her to-do list with a flourish. One done already.

Number two: write an introduction. And so it began. Hadley rolled her shoulders back, sat up straight in her chair, and started to type. She felt her own power start to flow from her fingers as she put words to the page. She didn't work particularly fast when she was writing. She liked to formulate the sentence in her head before typing it onto the page, but she was deliberate. When she finished, all that remained was a quick read-through for typos and minor rewordings, and then she could submit it with confidence. She had the whole process down to a science. On this, she knew herself very well.

She'd gotten through a page and a half when her carefully calculated plan was interrupted. Perhaps if she just hadn't looked up, she wouldn't have seen him, and she wouldn't have panicked, and she would have finished her essay on schedule. But at the very moment Jayden walked down the center path past her table, Hadley was taking a five-minute break. She was scrolling through the notifications on her phone—holding the screen up in front of her face because she had read it was better for her neck—when she saw a familiar figure striding past.

She glanced over automatically, and there he was. Jayden had his headphones on, eyes up, scanning the tables beyond for the best seat, so he didn't even see her where she sat on the far end by the bookshelves. But she sure saw him. He looked the same as he had over the summer, which shouldn't have surprised Hadley because it had only been a couple of months since she'd last seen him, but somehow she expected him to look different, changed, an exaggerated version of himself. She jerked her head back down and away from him.

Now was not the time. Hadley needed to be focused. She needed not to see him. He was farther down the row now, and he clearly hadn't seen her, but what if he did? What if he found a spot and turned around and saw her? Or what if he saw her when he left? She needed to be writing, her break time allotment was up, but her focus on her to-do list had vanished. She'd come to the library to write her paper and escape the worries and memories that were plaguing her, and instead, they—he—had followed her here. Now was not the time.

Hadley looked at her laptop, at the seven hundred words she'd written so far. Then she looked at her to-do list. Then she hazarded a glance up to see Jayden settling into a seat ten or so tables down.

She couldn't stay.

She flipped her laptop shut and undid each step of her unpacking process, this time at twice the speed. Her pencil went back in its pouch, the books back in her tote, followed by her planner and notebook. She wrapped up her charging cord and returned her laptop to its case. Less than two minutes after Jayden walked past her table, Hadley was speed-walking back out the way she'd come, jogging down the steps outside the library and hurrying toward her dorm. All she knew was she needed to be as far away as possible with the least chance of risking another encounter.

When she got back to her suite, Hadley collapsed onto the common room couch and tried to catch her breath, which she'd left somewhere back in the library.

"Hey, H." Bianca emerged from the hallway and gave her a once-over. "You look tired."

"You never fail to brighten my day, B," said Hadley. "I've just got a lot to do."

"Do you need snacks? Amy did a restock this morning."

"You read my mind," said Hadley, forcing a smile onto her face. She did need snacks, though. She got up to examine the shelf where she and her roommates kept their food and pulled out the box of Cheez-Its. "I might need to borrow this whole thing. I have a paper to write."

"Take it," said Bianca, waving her toward her room. "Are you going to need us to bring you dinner later?"

Hadley nodded, thanked her, then slipped into her room. She shut the door behind her and leaned against it, eyes closed, just for a moment.

It was a close call there in the library. Too close. She would need to be more careful to keep avoiding him. There were more obscure study spots on campus, she was sure. She'd never had to seek them out before, but perhaps this year was a good time to do so.

That was a problem for another day.

Hadley cracked open the box of Cheez-Its and shoveled a full handful into her mouth. She dropped her tote bag next to her desk and settled into the chair. She needed to get back her focus. She still had six and a half pages to write, and she had a feeling it was going to take a lot longer than it would've if she'd remained uninterrupted at the library.

She took a deep breath and pulled out her laptop.

8

JULY

"You look tired."

Jayden gently nudged Hadley with his elbow, jostling her from her reverie. She was leaning against the wall near the cafeteria entrance in the place that had become their unspoken meeting spot before lunch each day. He was giving her that half-smile of his, but he looked genuinely thoughtful as he appraised her demeanor.

"I'm exhausted," Hadley admitted, moving into step with him as they ambled toward the serving tables. "But I think it's mostly mental."

Jayden passed her a tray. "Anything worth sharing? Or are you just tired from throwing yourself into your work?"

Hadley forced a short laugh. "Just some stuff on my mind. It's nothing."

Jayden threw her a look as if trying to gauge how truthful she was being, but she turned toward the tray of french fries to avoid his gaze, and he seemed to accept her answer.

"Meet you outside?"

She nodded, and he headed for the noodles.

Hadley did have a lot on her mind. But it wasn't exactly nothing. In fact, it kind of felt like she had everything on her mind. The upcoming school year was fast approaching, and with it, a wave of existential dread about starting the second half of her college career. Two more years. Two more years until she needed to have a full-time job and pay bills and be on track for the rest of her life. But even that dread, like everything else these days, connected back to being at Vertex.

A month ago, she'd had no worries about the future. Honestly, it couldn't have arrived fast enough. After years of preparation, this summer at Vertex was supposed to be the true beginning of her career and her life, setting her up for a return offer or at least an impressive addition to her resume to help get her a job somewhere similar.

Marketing in the tech world was supposed to be her thing. It just made sense—the culmination of her studies in linguistics and the art of communication. Plus, it was a neat combination of what her parents did, and it made them proud. She'd grown up around tech people and marketing people, and even if Hadley hadn't necessarily seen herself as *one of them*, she knew she had the grit and the smarts to work with and through them. She was a future Chief Marketing Officer. That's always how she'd pictured herself, at the top of the game in her field, attending conferences and giving lectures in well-tailored high-end suits. That single image was what had driven her to keep her grades up, climb the ranks in her extracurriculars, and work a full-time retail job on top of an unpaid internship the previous summer to build up her resume. The problem now was that future seemed to be getting farther away, not closer. The path was getting less clear.

It wasn't that she didn't want that life anymore. She did want the success, the respect, and the glamour of being the very best at her job, but the years it would take to get there were giving her pause. And it wasn't because she was unwilling to work hard. She planned on working hard. It was more that she was no longer sure she would be happy, or even fine, doing the kind of work she would need to do to get there.

Hadley had seen what her supervisors did every day. Of course, they didn't come to work ecstatic about marketing and communications every single day. Still, she did see the way they got excited about good numbers and working on new campaigns, typing away with eyebrows furrowed in concentration, a smile playing on their lips as they found the perfect way to word a new ad. She noticed which assignments they assumed that she would be excited about, and she especially noticed she was never excited about them. She did the work, and while she never expected to be doing anything thrilling, she did expect to feel like this summer was the beginning of something good. And, more and more each day, she worried that feeling was never going to come.

Hadley glanced around the cafeteria, shoveling one last scoop of macaroni and cheese onto her plate. Jayden was still over in the corner perusing the dessert options, so she grabbed herself a set of silverware and headed for the door.

Jayden, too, had been on her mind recently. Over the last couple of weeks, he'd been a bit of a saving grace for her, even if he didn't know it. She wasn't sure if it was a good or a bad thing that he was the primary reason she looked forward to work at all these days, but he was. They ate lunch together every day, and she'd been suggesting some of her favorite restaurants for him to try so he could report back his reviews.

He was a breath of fresh air when she stepped away from her desk at noon each day. They never talked about work— maybe partially because of that contentious conversation on the first day they met, but mostly because Jayden had so many other things he was interested in talking to her about. They talked about school, of course, but he also wanted to know about where she grew up and what her family was like. She told him about her elementary school bully and how she became a bit of a mean girl herself in middle school until she found a new friend group in eighth grade. She even talked about how her determination to succeed in high school made her miss out on the occasional party and inadvertently distanced her from some of her friends, exercising a level of candor she hadn't expected herself to be comfortable with.

He asked her why she'd chosen the University of Seattle, and she said Seattle had felt like home the moment she stepped off the plane when she went to visit, and having tech companies like Microsoft and Amazon nearby had helped as she thought about her future. She talked about how she'd carefully planned her life to be in the tech world, though she didn't go into specifics. Jayden was a good listener, but she had a feeling he wouldn't be so approving if she told him she'd basically specifically selected every class and every extracurricular in order to secure this exact internship this summer.

Jayden's approach to life was a near opposite to Hadley's. He was smart—that much was clear—but his perspective on working and his future was nothing like hers. His primary motivation for coming to Vertex this summer was to stay on the West Coast instead of going home to Chicago and to make good money while he could. He planned to travel for a year after graduation in the spring, while he was still "young enough to make dumb decisions," as he said, staying in hostels and taking trains across Europe—the whole deal—and then start working in the public sector. He told her he wanted to make life better. That was the only thing he really knew for sure.

Hadley admired his desire to help people and his laissez-faire attitude toward life. He was unabashed about taking advantage of the opportunity to work at Vertex, gaining experience and money for his year abroad, and then happy to leave the corporate world behind. But she was also intimidated by his casual confidence. It was a stark contrast to her carefully constructed veneer of confidence that was anything but casual. She didn't think her plan to force herself into a world she didn't really care about would impress him very much, and she certainly wasn't going to jeopardize her only genuine companion for the summer. So far, the other interns didn't seem like her kind of people, and she had taken refuge in her friendship with Jayden.

Jayden dropped his tray next to Hadley's and she looked up with a start.

"If you could only eat one color of food for the rest of your life, what color would you choose?" he asked.

She blushed, embarrassed she'd been reminiscing so extensively on their friendship up until that moment. "What?"

"You can only eat food of one color for the rest of your life. Red, green, purple, what do you choose?"

Hadley carefully considered the question. She looked down at her plate and over at Jayden's. "Yellow."

"Interesting. Why?"

"There's a decent variety of options to cover every food group. You get pasta and bread. Some vegetables—yellow carrots, corn, yellow peppers, squash, potatoes." She gestured to the french fries on her plate. "For protein, you could have some fish, maybe tofu. A handful of desserts. Lots of fruit. You could still eat pretty balanced."

Jayden was looking at her, a small smile playing on his lips.

"What's that look for?" she asked, laughing.

"You're just funny," he said. "I should've guessed you'd pick something like that."

"What do you mean?"

"It's just a very logical answer."

"Oh? And what would you pick?" she asked.

"Brown," said Jayden, leaning back in his seat with his arms crossed over his chest. "Steaks, chocolate, and brown bread. The good stuff."

"And I should've guessed you'd pick something indulgent like that." Hadley laughed again.

"If I only get to eat one color, I'd better enjoy the options." Jayden shrugged, grinning.

Hadley loved when Jayden came up with random topics of conversation like this. She liked having the opportunity to break out of her perpetual focus on the future and into the space of the imaginary, the hypothetical, even just the true present. He gave her something else to think about. For a full three minutes, she had stopped worrying about her future and was able to be truly present. She craved that levity. She craved being able to forget about the weight on her mind, even for just a minute. She didn't want to lose that feeling.

"What are you doing this weekend?" she asked too loudly as if the impulse burst from her lips entirely on its own.

"What are you thinking?" said Jayden.

"I don't know, but we should do something."

"An adventure." Jayden smiled.

"Anything," said Hadley.

9

OCTOBER

Hadley was starting to get nervous. Things were starting to pile up on her to-do list, to the point where the likelihood of completing some assignments by the due dates was stretching the realm of possibility. And she wasn't exactly sure why or how things had gotten to this point. Sure, perhaps the extra measures to avoid Jayden and find new places to study were taking up some of her time, but so were her therapy sessions, and she hadn't been expecting the junior year workload to jump up quite so much. It was getting a bit nerve-wracking, trying to manage it all, not to mention she was still trying to have some semblance of a social life—going to the occasional party or football game with Bianca and Amy. She supposed everyone had these moments when a million things were going on, and of course, she had experienced this before, during college application season and internship recruitment season.

Speaking of which, internship recruitment season had long since begun for many of her peers, so finding a job for next summer was becoming a preoccupation of Hadley's on top of everything else. The problem was she wasn't exactly sure where to begin. She felt like she was starting over, which was a daunting thought. She didn't know where to be looking. What sector? What kinds of positions? What kinds of companies? She knew she should probably make an appointment at the Career Center, but the idea of having to sit down and explain what was going on and how lost she felt was more than a little off-putting.

Hadley glanced down at her phone to check the time and gave a start. She was going to be late for her appointment with Angie. She packed up her belongings, clearing off the table in the lounge she'd newly discovered on the second floor of the math building.

What was Angie going to ask her about today? To be honest, she wasn't entirely upset about the fact she was going to be late. It meant she'd gotten a few extra minutes of work in, and she would have less time to spend in that bright little office. It wasn't that she minded, really, having to go to therapy, and she knew where her parents were coming from in mandating the visits, but she mostly felt like there were better uses of her time. Hadley wasn't a huge fan of talking about her feelings with other people, especially when she didn't even know how to articulate them to herself. And Angie was always pressing her to think more critically about how she acted and who she spent her time with and why, and she honestly didn't think it was working. Perhaps therapy just wasn't for her. Besides, she knew exactly what needed to get done in order to get back to being her usual self. She needed to focus on school, her classes, and her extracurriculars and figure out what she would do next in terms of her career path. Once she had that sorted, she could focus on achieving her goal. Hadley was good at that. She was good at to-do lists and planning, and getting where she needed to go.

Right now, she just needed a destination. And she knew she wasn't going to find it on Angie's blue chaise longue.

Regardless of how she felt, she had an appointment, and though she was happy to shave a few minutes off of her hour, she couldn't stop a flash of anxiety about her lateness from racing through her as she hurried toward the mental health clinic. She wasn't normally one to be late. Or early, for that matter. She liked to be right on time. At least her excuse was an honest one.

She jogged the last few steps into the building and hit the elevator up button three times. When she walked into the clinic, she strode purposefully toward the front desk—a seasoned client.

"I'm here to see Dr. Rowe. I'm a little late, I lost track of—"

"I'll let her know," said the receptionist, waving her off. "You can take a seat."

Hadley had hardly sat down when Angie popped her head around the corner, her usual smile on her face. "Hey, Hadley, come on in."

Hadley settled into her spot on the little couch. "I'm sorry I'm late. I lost track of time."

"It happens," Angie replied. "I'm glad you're here." She crossed her legs and balanced her notepad on her knee. "Do you want to share what you've been up to since we last spoke?"

"I've been good," Hadley said. "Pretty busy. I just came from doing homework, that's why I was late. There's a lot going on right now."

"Like what?"

"Just lots of work. Junior year is definitely keeping me busy. Lots of assignments to stay on top of and extracurriculars and everything. It definitely feels like the most work I've ever had. So I'm just trying to buckle down and get through it."

"Does it worry you? Trying to keep track of everything? I can imagine it would be stressful keeping up with all that." Angie smiled at Hadley, her pen poised over her notepad.

It always bugged Hadley when Angie did that, held her pen up, expectant, just waiting for her to say something revealing about her psyche. "I guess. I mean, there's always some stress at school, especially when things start to pile up. I feel like I work best when I'm under pressure. Always have. So I'm not too worried. I know myself and how I work. I just have to stick to my normal strategies."

"What kinds of strategies are those?"

"My study strategies. Lots of to-do lists and keeping track of things in my planner. It helps to have everything written down and then plan out what I need to get done each day."

"That sounds like a good strategy. What's your strategy for managing stress? How do you keep yourself calm with so many things going on?"

Hadley thought about it. She wasn't sure what kind of answer Angie was looking for. "I think the best thing for me is to just get things done. Once I turn in an assignment or complete a task, I don't have to worry about it anymore. So my study strategies are kind of the same thing as my stress relief strategies."

"Does that seem like enough to you? Enough to keep your stress levels low?" Angie was writing something down. Hadley was itching to get her hands on that notepad.

"It's worked for me so far."

Angie was still writing. Maybe she should add something else. She didn't want her therapist to think she was some sort of a workaholic. "I hang out with friends, too. I always take time on weekends to do something fun with my roommates. I set aside time for that."

"That sounds nice. What kinds of things do you like to do with them?"

"We go out sometimes or go to a sports game of some sort. We also like to have nights in and get takeout or watch something together. That sort of thing."

Angie wrote down one last thing and looked up at Hadley. "It sounds like you have some good strategies. I'm glad to hear you feel like you're able to manage your stress and workload. Is there anything, in particular, that's bothering you that you'd like to talk about today? It can be related to schoolwork or not. I know I always say this, but this is really your time to bring up anything you want."

Hadley wondered if anything *was* bothering her in particular. There was Jayden, for one, who she'd successfully been able to avoid since the near encounter in the library, but the fear of running into him again definitely hung around in the back of her mind most of the time. And then there was her future, which, more than bothering her, was starting to scare her. But she could picture Angie scribbling down all of her concerns on that mysterious notepad, that calm and kind look on her face, and that bothered her more than anything. That definitely would not help assuage her stress.

"Not in particular," she said. "The usual. Midterms are coming up and everything, so that will be a heavier workload."

"I can see how that would make you a little apprehensive. Do you want to talk about any specific strategies to handle that? If you expect your workload to increase, how do you plan to mitigate that?"

Hadley relaxed a little bit, letting her back sink into the sofa. This she would happily discuss. At least more happily than some of the other things Angie seemed to want to pry out of her. She could definitely get through at least twenty minutes of just talking about her plans to front-load her homework, get ahead on her readings, and meet with her professors early to leave plenty of breathing room around midterms. Angie seemed content with the kinds of things they were discussing now. Hadley thought an extra level of detail or two about her study habits could get her through the rest of her appointment without having to delve into anything Angie deemed more important than her mental wellbeing. Then, after she got out of her appointment, she had an hour and a half to work before her next meeting. She tried to picture her to-do list. What could she get done in that time?

"I've been thinking about that," she said. "And I have a few good strategies."

10

———

When Hadley's alarm went off on Saturday morning, she snoozed it three times. She checked her phone once she finally sat herself up and already had a text from Jayden. The text was a screenshot of the weather forecast, hot and sunny all day, accompanied by a palm tree and a swimming emoji. Nerves were knotted in the pit of her stomach by the time she dragged herself out of bed.

Standing in front of the bathroom mirror, Hadley forced herself to take deep breaths in an attempt to alleviate the nausea rising in her throat. She just needed to hold it together, to get herself in check. She was not unfamiliar with this feeling. Much the same as the one she got around finals week or the day her college decisions came out or pretty much any time she had very little clothing on around other people. Her familiarity, however, didn't stop her from running through every potential excuse she could use to get out of this trip to the beach.

She could say she slept through her alarm or was feeling sick. That much was true. There was really nothing Jayden could say or do if she conjured up a family emergency or told him her parents were making her run errands all day. It wasn't that she didn't want to see him. She wanted to see him very much, but for the first time, she felt like today was maybe a date. Sure, they ate lunch together, and he was basically the only person she talked to at work, but this was a real excursion—all the way to the beach.

And a date in a swimsuit? Even the thought of it made the knot in her stomach tighten. Best-case scenario, he would cancel on her, which would make it much easier for her to distance herself from him in turn, and then perhaps the whole thing would fade away, and on campus, in the fall, they would just wave at each other from afar. She was starting to convince herself she might actually be sick, and she really did need to stay in bed all day. Besides, after all this time hanging out as friends, Jayden would probably be let down by her companionship outside of the work setting. At Vertex, they were surrounded by the tech-types that Jayden didn't even like, so he'd befriended Hadley almost by default. What an awkward conversation it would be when he realized he didn't actually think she was all that great. Better to avoid the situation altogether.

But Jayden didn't text her to cancel. And the more time passed as Hadley made herself breakfast and ate it in front of an episode of *The Great British Baking Show*, the more rude and awkward and unconvincing she felt it would be for her to come up with an excuse not to go. Finally, it was ten minutes before she was supposed to leave to pick him up, so the only thing she could think to do was to change into her most flattering bikini, put a sundress on over it, and slip out the back door to avoid any unwanted questions from her parents in the living room.

In the car, she tried playing calming music and taking deep breaths, even though she knew from experience the only thing that would really alleviate her stress was seeing Jayden and demonstrating to herself that the day would not be as awkward as she feared. She wished she could talk herself into believing today was no different than any of their lunches. She'd spent plenty of time talking to him then, and she could do it today, too. But leaving the work-affiliated safety of the Vertex headquarters felt like stepping outside a safety bubble. Yes, they had spent time together, but there was always an implicit excuse that it was because neither of the two of them had much in common with anyone else at work. Today, going to the beach together, they were admitting perhaps they shared something more than a distaste for their coworkers.

He was already waiting outside when she arrived, sitting on the stoop of his apartment building, leaning back with his elbows propped on the step behind him—the picture of ease. He was clearly not afflicted by nerves of any kind, a realization which Hadley hoped would signal to her stomach knot that it could untangle itself.

Jayden smiled when he saw her pull up to the curb. "HD!" he called out—more directed to the universe than to her and attracting the glances of a few passersby.

Hadley felt a rush of heat in her cheeks that, surprisingly, seemed to have more to do with a thrill in her chest than with embarrassment. He was casually handsome in board shorts and a white t-shirt, a curl or two dangling in front of his eyes. He strode toward the car, and watching him approach, Hadley allowed herself to realize the physical stress of the morning had just as much to do with excitement as with worry.

"Ready for this?" Jayden asked as he slid into the passenger seat beside her, dropping a drawstring bag onto the floor between his legs. Despite everything, nausea, the lethargy, and the urge to call it all off, Hadley was ready. She pulled away from the curb as Jayden leaned his seat back and popped open the sunroof, making himself at home in a way only he could.

The first minutes of the drive passed in relative silence after Hadley and Jayden exchanged pleasantries, asking about each other's mornings. Hadley pretended to be very focused on driving as if she hadn't driven to this very beach innumerable times before.

The last time she'd been was the previous summer. She and her high school friends had packed a picnic, as they had done so many times in their late teens, and piled into Hadley's car for a day in the sun. Though none of them would say it out loud, or even to themselves, the excursion had really been an attempt to recapture what had made them all so close in high school. An attempt to prove they hadn't grown apart as much as it seemed. If anything, however, their nostalgic beach day proved the exact opposite.

The first hour or so had flown by fairly easily, as all of them were able to reminisce over the times they'd spent on the beach together. Toes buried deep in the sand, gossiping about high school drama, the sunscreen they'd promised their moms to bring left untouched at the bottom of their bags. But once they'd talked through all of the memories, the changes in all of them were impossible to ignore. It wasn't necessarily that they had nothing to talk about, but the things they were each interested in talking about no longer overlapped nearly as much as they had when they were all spending five days a week in the same building and seven days a week in the same city.

Maggie was deeply involved in her sorority, and it showed. Her hair had gotten at least four shades lighter since initiation, and she managed to bring any topic of conversation back around to some party she'd been to, the drama in the sorority house, or a frat boy she'd gone to a formal with. Piper took the previous semester off from school for her mental health and worked on a political campaign. Hadley was actually interested to hear about it, but she got so sick of Piper's condescending looks when she didn't know the details of a proposed policy or the name of the Democratic senator from Arizona that she stared intently at her phone until Piper got the hint and turned away.

Hadley's focus, too, had changed. In high school, her goal had been to fit in and set herself up well for college. Now that she had achieved that—graduating with all As and getting into the rigorous University of Seattle—she set her sights on her career and what came next. She just didn't have much in common with her high school friends anymore. They had each gone away to college and found their people. The truth of the matter was they had all grown into themselves in the last few years, but the hard part to admit was that the people they were now didn't have the same taste in shoes, dates, or friends that they'd had in high school.

"Did you go to this beach very often growing up?" Jayden's question jerked Hadley back to the present. He was always perceptive, but the timeliness of his question was a little strange even for him. She must have given him a look of confusion because he added, "You mentioned you're from nearby."

"Right. Yeah, sometimes." Hadley felt a little stab of sorrow in her chest as she glossed over the many years of memories she'd made at this particular beach. She liked this one because it was generally quieter than the more popular beaches, but she didn't want Jayden to think she was taking him to a special place of hers and draw any conclusions. Better to make it all as casual as possible.

"If I lived near beaches like the ones here, I would be there every day." Hadley glanced over at Jayden, trying to gauge whether his comment was a dig, though that didn't seem like his style. He was gazing out the window, his tone wistful. "It's not the same in the Midwest."

"What do you mean?"

Jayden seemed to shake himself, sitting up straighter. "Oh, I just like the vibe of the West Coast, that's all. It feels free. I didn't realize how much I was going to like it out here."

Hadley's first inclination was to be surprised it was Jayden's first time on this corner of the country, but she supposed, having lived here all her life, California felt ubiquitous to her. "You can always move here after graduation," she said, tentative. She wasn't sure exactly what Jayden wanted to hear. "Maybe not to Vertex, but you could get a job somewhere else."

"Maybe." He gave her a small smile. "Mostly, I think I realize how much more of the world there is to see. Maybe going into the workforce straight out of college isn't for me."

"And do what instead? All I want is to have a job waiting for me after graduation. It would make my life so much easier if I could avoid the whole application process and just come back here to Vertex. That's what I've been hoping for," Hadley said, even though she wasn't sure she really was hoping for that anymore. She figured almost anyone would want a return offer from Vertex, and at this point, she really didn't know what she wanted exactly, so there was no point in trying to explain.

"I just want to see more of what's out there before I lock myself into any one thing. But who knows? It feels hard to justify when working seems like the normal and responsible option, but maybe it's worth shocking a couple of people to be able to do some more exploring."

Hadley nodded, even though she didn't totally understand what he was saying. If anyone could throw convention out the window to do whatever he wanted, however, she thought that would be Jayden.

"We're getting close," she said. And they were. The buildings were getting shorter, and they could smell the ocean in the air rushing through the open windows.

Jayden leaned forward into the seat, closing his eyes to take a deep inhale. "So we are."

As Hadley had hoped, the beach was sparsely populated, and she and Jayden had an ample swath of sand to themselves. She laid out the two beach towels she'd brought from home because Jayden didn't have any in his rented summer apartment. In exchange, he'd agreed to bring the snacks.

Jayden stretched his arms, gazing out at the expanse of the ocean in front of them. "We have to get in there," he said. In one swift motion, he pulled off his shirt, discarded it on his towel, and started jogging toward the water. "Come on, HD!"

He didn't even give Hadley enough time to be self-conscious. She dropped her dress coverup and ran after him, not wanting to be left behind. She ran in up to her knees, giving a small shriek at the cold ocean water. But Jayden didn't give her enough time to do her usual wade-in tactic either. She'd barely come to a stop before he splashed her stomach with a sheet of water.

"Jayden!" she yelled.

"You just have to get in!" he said. When he turned around to move farther out, she splashed him in the back.

"Hey!" he said. "I was trying to do you a favor!"

"And I'm just trying to return it," Hadley replied. She saw an evil glint in his eye and started to do that awkward high-knee run through the water to get away from him, to no avail. Within moments, they were both entirely soaked, squinting to try to keep the salt out of their eyes, but they were laughing.

"Let's swim out," said Jayden.

Hadley glanced back at their towels and bags, left unguarded on the sand. She only hesitated for a moment, however, before turning back and swimming after Jayden.

They swam out until they couldn't see the faces of the people on the beach. Hadley could still see their towels, though— two red squares against the beige expanse.

"What a life," said Jayden, floating on the surface of the water, face toward the sky.

"It's a special place," said Hadley absentmindedly, thinking back again to the many memories she'd made here.

"I can see that," he said, gently skimming his arms over the surface of the water to keep himself afloat. "Are any of your friends back here for the summer, too?"

Maggie was, and maybe Quinn, too. "Not really." She didn't want to explain the whole drifting apart thing. Jayden didn't seem like the type to just let go of old friends as she had. To avoid any further questions, Hadley spun herself around in the water and kept swimming out toward the point. Jayden followed, and they swam in comfortable silence—save for the sound of their arms slicing through the waves—until Hadley started to worry if they went any farther, they would run out of energy to get back.

"I'm hungry," she said.

"Good thing I stocked up on snacks this morning," said Jayden, even though Hadley was already swimming back toward the shore. As she got closer, she let the waves push her toward the beach until her feet hit the sand.

Back on land, Jayden pulled packages of sliced grocery store fruit and bags of chips from his backpack as Hadley wrapped herself in her towel. Away from the carefree magic of the ocean, she remembered all the parts of her body she would rather he didn't see. They snacked in silence for a while. The exhaustion of their swim was just beginning to sink in. Hadley could feel herself closing up, her openness drying up with the saltwater on her body.

"What are you doing later?" Jayden asked.

Hadley felt her nausea from the morning begin to creep up her throat. Today had been good— the perfect distraction from her worries. The last thing she needed was the stress of an evening portion of their maybe-date. "I have to be home by dinner," she said, reaching for her dress to pull it back over her head. She saw Jayden's face fall just the slightest amount, and she couldn't help but feel glad he was disappointed to cut the day short. "But maybe we can stay here a little longer."

11

JULY

"What are you doing after work?"

Hadley whipped around at the sound of Jayden's voice. He had come up behind her in the hall where she was bent over the water fountain, a big grin on his face. She had only seen him in his swim trunks that once, but it was still somehow off-putting to see him back in his work polo and shorts.

It was the Monday after their beach day, and Hadley and Jayden had taken the miraculous step of sitting with another group of interns at lunch, pushing themselves to interact with their peers but losing the chance to debrief their excursion to the ocean.

"What are you doing on my floor?" she teased, wiping the water where it had dripped onto her chin with her sleeve. "You scared me."

"We didn't get a chance to talk much at lunch," he said. "It was weird. So what are you doing after work?"

"Why?" She narrowed her eyes at him and gave him a small smile. "Did you have something in mind?"

"Not in particular. But I can't just go home. I need to do something." He nudged her with his elbow. "And I don't have a car."

"Oh, I see," said Hadley, feigning offense. "You're just using me for my car. First for the beach and now for a Monday whim."

He grinned wider if that was possible. "Maybe. But that's not the only reason I'm asking you."

Hadley wanted to press him, to make him tell her what he meant, but she couldn't muster the confidence. Jayden made her feel comfortable for the most part, but she felt like asking a follow-up question would edge into foreign territory, and she didn't want to be the one to lead the way there.

"Well, I'm free." She hoped she didn't sound overly eager.

"I'll meet you after work, then," said Jayden, clasping his hands in front of him. He looked suddenly rather awkward as if he didn't quite know what else to say, which definitely was not his normal state.

Hadley gave him a bright smile. "I'll text you when I'm headed to the lobby."

He smiled back.

Hadley gave him a small wave and returned to her desk, a nervous sort of flutter billowing in her chest. What did this mean? Did he really want to catch up from lunch, or was he looking to continue what she had cut off so abruptly at the beach? Either way, he wanted to spend more time with her, and he was making it happen. She appreciated his initiative in coming to find her during the workday. However, it did demonstrate a concerning lack of commitment to the sort of steadfast work ethic of most of their Vertex intern peers. Who was she kidding? She was thrilled to see him.

This was good. It had been a grueling start to the week. Hadley was overwhelmed with spreadsheets to sift through, putting the Excel skills she had generously given herself on her resume to the test. She needed a distraction.

———

Jayden was already waiting on one of the lobby couches when Hadley emerged from the stairwell. He couldn't have been waiting long, but he had made himself comfortable. One leg stretched out on the couch, his laptop opened on his lap, and what looked like most of the contents of his backpack scattered across the coffee table.

"Don't get up on my account," she said, laughing, as she approached.

He looked up, dazed. "There you are." Jayden looked around at the items splayed about. He laughed. "I guess I kind of made myself at home."

"You tend to do that, you know. Make yourself at home."

"Is that a bad thing?" He smiled.

"No, it isn't. But can you do it in my car? Let's get out of here." Hadley motioned toward the door and started to walk in its direction, eager to be done with Vertex for the day.

Jayden scooped everything back into his backpack and jogged after her. "That bad, huh?"

Hadley looked back at him as she stepped through the doors. She shrugged. "Not the most enthralling projects. Let's not talk about it."

Jayden didn't press her, instead explaining the entire premise of a new Netflix reality show that he couldn't stop watching as they walked to the car. He was moving on to give her a rundown of each cast member and their dramatic contributions as they buckled their seatbelts.

"Where to?" said Hadley, interrupting Jayden's explanation, though she was actually enjoying this unexpected dramatic flair.

"Surprise me." He paused. "But I'm hungry."

"I know just the place."

Hadley pulled out of the parking lot, flipping down the sun visor as they turned into the early evening glare. The streets shone golden as they drove through the back roads, past corner stores, family-owned boutiques, and kids playing soccer in front of their houses. In fifteen minutes, they were shifting into park outside Hadley's favorite taco truck, unassumingly tucked into the corner of the wide parking lot shared with a gas station and a convenience store. The truck itself was large, plastered with pictures of the taco and beverage options that were labeled by hand. It was the kind of place where the looks belied the tastiness of the food. Hadley could smell it before she even opened the car door. Two construction workers were sitting in the back of a pickup nearby, eating out of plastic containers.

"Trust me," said Hadley as she turned off the engine, "these will change your life."

"Lead the way," said Jayden.

The mouth-watering aroma tantalized them as they approached the truck, the scent of roasting meat and the sizzle of the grill drowning out the ambiance of the nearby gas station.

"What are you going to get?" Hadley asked.

Jayden scanned the photos that bordered the order window. "Order me something," he said finally. "I trust you."

Hadley didn't hesitate. If there was only one thing she could do with confidence these days, it was order tacos.

"Let me get it," Jayden said as she reached for her wallet. "I owe you for gas money."

Hadley shook her head. "No, no, I picked the place. It's on me." She started to pull out her card, but Jayden covered her hand with his. It was warm but not uncomfortably so.

"I'm the one who wanted to get something to eat. You wouldn't be here if I hadn't insisted. I'll get it."

"You don't know that," said Hadley, eyebrows raised. "I come here at least once a week." But she didn't stop him from offering up a couple of bills through the window. "Thank you," she said.

"Thanks for driving," said Jayden. Within minutes, they were walking back to the car with two warm containers of tacos and two sodas.

"Do you want to eat here?" Hadley asked. "We could just sit in the car."

Jayden looked around as if to see whether there were any seating options nearby. There weren't.

"We're not far from my apartment, right? You would know better than me."

Hadley nodded.

"I don't have a ton of space, but there's a table," said Jayden.

"Sounds good," said Hadley as she tried not to let herself get too nervous. Now, what did *this* mean? First, he wanted to hang out with her after work, and now he was inviting her back to his apartment? Sure, maybe it really just was out of convenience, but he could have just agreed to eat in her car. It had to mean *something*. She wasn't quite sure how to act as she maneuvered out of the parking lot and turned on to the street. *Act casual.*

Jayden's apartment building was aging but well-kept, with neat hedges lining the front walkway. He led the way up the steps, through the double doors, up the elevator, and down the slim, dimly lit hallway to his rental. He unlocked the door and held it open for her.

As he had said, the space was small but functional and clean. To the immediate right of the entry was a kitchenette tucked into one corner. Between the open kitchen area and the living space directly ahead was the table in question, five books stacked on its surface—an eclectic mix of nonfiction and sci-fi.

"Let me get those out of the way," he said, transferring the stack to the coffee table between the short couch and armchair.

"This is nice," said Hadley, doing her best not to make it obvious she was trying to catch a glimpse of the bedroom through the cracked door. It looked neat and sparse from the slim triangle she could see.

"It works," he replied. "Vertex helped cover it. I think there might be a couple of other interns in the building. Not that I've been particularly proactive about trying to meet them, but I see them on the shuttle." He motioned for her to sit down at the table.

Hadley cracked open both of the plastic containers. "One is al pastor, and one is chicken. You should try both."

They tucked in, and the conversation ceased for a while, except for a few exclamations at the flavor from Jayden's side of the table. Hadley took her time, pouring salsa and squeezing lime onto each taco and enjoying each bite with her eyes closed. This was what Hadley needed. A break from work, from the slog through the summer. She didn't want to think too much about it, but as she sat chewing and silence started to fill the space between her and Jayden, she couldn't stop the thoughts and fears from trickling back in. There was so much to think about, so much to figure out. This was the career path she had chosen, the dream company she had pursued, and she couldn't give up on it now, could she? That would mean starting from scratch, finding a new dream. She couldn't afford that.

She finished her last taco and started wiping her mouth and fingers with a napkin. But, on the other hand, she couldn't imagine herself getting through a couple of years of this same kind of thing in an entry-level position. She couldn't even imagine convincing a recruiter she wanted to do marketing again for next summer.

"That was crazy," said Jayden, loading their soiled napkins and empty soda bottles into the empty containers.

Hadley was starting to feel a little crazy. She needed to stop thinking about this. She needed to be distracted. The afternoon had gone so well so far, and this excursion had been her motivation to get through the last few hours of work since Jayden had appeared behind her at the water fountain. But there were still so many answers she didn't have about the future. She needed to stop thinking entirely.

Jayden was looking at her expectantly, waiting for a response or the start of a new conversation. Instead, she leaned across the table and kissed him. Not for too long, but firmly. Inexplicably, she felt the tightness in her chest start to release, and her mind go almost blank. Almost. Sitting there, kissing Jayden, Hadley felt happier than she had all summer. For a moment, she thought it was perhaps the boldest thing she'd ever done.

"Oh," said Jayden.

"Yeah," said Hadley, flushing.

A slow smile spread across Jayden's face. He leaned in to kiss her again, and, as she pulled away, Hadley found she couldn't even remember the name of the company where they worked.

12

OCTOBER

The peak noise levels in the stadium surprised Hadley every time, regardless of how many games she'd attended there in her years of college. The roar of several thousand students, alums, and loyal locals assaulted her eardrums as she, Bianca, and Amy slid into their row well into the second quarter.

"There you are!" Mika, Bianca's ex from freshman year who'd managed to remain good friends with all of them, threw up her hands, accidentally splashing some of the contents of her drink on the guy in the row in front of her, but he was far too drunk to even register the spill. "Please don't tell me you guys are sober. I can't believe you missed the tailgate."

Sebastian leaned around her to look at the new arrivals. "What's the point of coming to a football game if you don't go to the tailgate?"

"Don't worry," said Amy, hugging Mika. "We slept in nice and late and then pregamed in our cozy little common room instead of in a parking lot."

"The alcohol is definitely kicking in," said Bianca, fanning her face with her hand. She squeezed past Mika and

Sebastian to dole out greetings to the rest of their friends down the row.

"How's the game?" Hadley asked. She turned to look at the scoreboard, the beer and three vodka shots making her vision slow as the alcohol swirled in her head. Their team was down by four, but they had the ball.

"A couple of bad plays," said Mika. "That sophomore receiver has been getting all the hype, but he has no hands."

"Apparently, someone's been watching," Sebastian chimed in, nudging Mika with his elbow. "I just cheer when everyone else does."

"Your lack of school pride is embarrassing," Mika chided him.

"I have school pride!" Sebastian gestured to his bright blue logo sweatshirt.

"He has school pride for the tailgates, just not so much for the games themselves," said Hadley, laughing.

This was exactly the kind of day Hadley needed. Out with friends, tipsy enough to let her guard down and socialize, anonymous in a sea of thousands of people. Just another dumb drunk student.

The problem was, she was having a hard time buying into the whole thing. Sure the alcohol was helping, but her stress levels were sobering, to say the least. Despite the elaborate plan she had laid out for Angie, her midterm assignments had started sneaking up on her. She wasn't ahead on her readings—in fact, she was a little behind—and the prospect of two upcoming midterm exams and several papers was more than a little daunting. She felt like she hardly got done with one thing before two more deadlines materialized on her calendar. She did her best to put it out of her mind.

"First down!" Mika shouted as the crowd cheered.

Hadley clapped her hands and yelled along with the rest of them, but she was starting to question her decision to trek out to the stadium in the cold, not quite drunk enough to forget the responsibilities she was foregoing to be here.

The rest of the game dragged on. Once the thought of her deadlines drifted into her head, she couldn't get it out again. The temporary reprieve afforded by an hour of drinking and blasting music in the common room with her roommates dissipated in the chilly autumn air. She hardly registered when the opposing team scored another field goal, the boos of her peers falling on preoccupied ears.

Hadley and Amy briefly escaped the biting wind to buy chicken tenders and french fries from the concession stand at halftime.

"Are you okay?" Amy asked as they loaded their food with condiments pumped out of giant plastic bottles.

Hadley looked up with a start. "What do you mean?"

Amy was looking at her with some concern and also a nontrivial amount of discomfort. Amy was always perceptive, but she didn't often voice her observations. Normally, if she noticed something was off with Hadley or Bianca, she would quietly leave a bar of chocolate or bag of Hot Cheetos on their bed, occasionally with a note of encouragement. She didn't often bring these things up.

"I'm… I guess it just seems like you have a lot on your plate. You're always busy, but these days you seem extra busy."

Hadley was surprised. Less because Amy was saying something, but more so because of what it meant. If Amy was saying she seemed busy, what she meant was she seemed stressed, and Hadley wasn't the type to show her stress. This little comment meant something was slipping. Something was showing. She couldn't have that happen. This semester was her chance to prove—to the universe, her family, Jayden, and herself—she could recover from the summer and get back to being her usual high-functioning self.

"I'm fine," she replied quickly. "Lots going on, but that's life." She laughed. "Midterms coming up and everything. What about you? Lots of exams?" She hoped turning the tables would make Amy think she'd been wrong in her perception. She just had to make it all seem casual, normal.

Amy gave her a tentative smile. "Yeah, lots of exams." She paused. "Well, I'm glad. That you're good, that's good." Hadley thought she saw her friend's cheeks turn a little pink. "And I'm glad you came to the game today. We all need to be getting out of the room a little more."

Amy was telling Hadley she needed to be getting out of the room a *lot* more. She spoke as if she were talking about all of them, but she really meant Hadley. Hadley took a mental note. She'd been spending so much time in the room between all her schoolwork, extracurricular work, and avoiding Jayden that Amy had noticed and thought something was wrong. Well, she certainly didn't want her thinking that. She would need to be more cognizant. She could spend a little more time seeking out those new, unconventional study spots where she could tackle her work without the threat of Jayden materializing somewhere nearby.

Hadley nodded her agreement as she grabbed a handful of napkins from the dispenser. "I'm so hungry," she said. Amy reached over and snatched one of her chicken tenders out of her container. "Hey!"

Amy took a big bite and almost spat it out. "Hot!" she said, mouth hanging open as if the air could help cool down her singed tongue.

"That's what you get," said Hadley, holding her tenders close to her chest as she and Amy made their way back to their seats and their friends.

Hadley hoped she'd eased Amy's mind. The last thing she needed, on top of everything else, was the additional worry about appeasing her friend. She was fine. She just needed time to figure things out by herself. If only Angie could see that too.

The three roommates, along with a smattering of their friends, left the game early, partway into the fourth quarter, when the home team was up by enough they didn't really have to worry about taking their lucky energy with them out of the stadium. Their friends wanted to have enough time to warm up, get changed, and grab dinner before going out again later that night. Amy and Bianca had expressed enthusiasm at that plan, particularly the part about warming up and going out to party. Hadley had gone along with it, happy to get back to their cozy room and curl up into some sweatpants.

"What time do you guys want to go out later?" Bianca asked as they hurried into the lobby of their dorm building. "Mika said we could go over to her place to top up on alcohol."

"Ooh, you want to hang out with Mika?" Amy started to giggle. "You guys were talking a lot at the game."

Bianca rolled her eyes. "Can't we just be good friends?"

"I don't think so," said Amy.

"You would know," said Hadley. "You couldn't stay out of Peter's room for three weeks after you broke up."

All three of them started to laugh, but, despite her joke, Hadley was still thinking about how the evening was going to go. She wasn't particularly thrilled about the idea of going out and taking even more hours out of her day. She needed to be working and catching up on things to put herself in the best position for the weeks to come. Besides, she had been planning on doing some research on the Career Center website about how best to find potential job options. There were a million things for her to be doing, and drinking for the second time in one day certainly wasn't one of them. But as she walked into the common room, a pensive look on her face, she saw Amy glance over at her.

She didn't want Amy to worry. If she told them she didn't want to go out tonight, Amy would definitely start worrying again. She already thought Hadley didn't get out of the room enough. What would she think if she turned down a night out so soon after their conversation at the stadium? The other option was to fake a non-school-related excuse for staying in. Illness? Period cramps? That wouldn't work on them. Bianca would definitely tell her to take an Ibuprofen and suck it up. Anyway, above all else, Hadley was mentally exhausted. The easiest thing was to just go out and deal with the consequences of schoolwork tomorrow.

"Can I tell Mika we'll be over in an hour and a half?" Bianca asked, pushing open the door to their suite.

Amy looked over at Hadley.

"Definitely," said Hadley.

13

___

AUGUST

Hadley felt like she was on a perpetual rollercoaster of emotions. Ever since their first kiss on Monday, she'd been overwhelmingly happy when she got to spend time with Jayden at lunch and occasionally after work, but that elation dissipated just as quickly whenever they weren't together. Work was getting worse. The more hours she spent at that desk in the middle of the flex space, the more she felt like she was going to lose her mind. She had finally begun to admit to herself she really hated what she was doing, but that admission didn't help her figure out what to do.

Was it the company she didn't like? But that couldn't be possible. Vertex was everyone's dream company. It would be such a rush to drop that name when she got back to campus and people asked her what she'd done over the summer. Was it the department then? Or marketing in general? That was almost worse. This summer was the product of countless hours of unpaid internships coupled with retail jobs to earn some money, volunteer positions and extracurricular leadership roles for her resume, and classes for her transcript. A realization marketing was the thing making her so unhappy would spell the end of everything she'd worked toward. That would mean starting over. And how would she even begin to do that?

The only thing to do was to get through this summer and then reevaluate. She could find somewhere else to work next summer. Then she wouldn't have to worry about getting a return offer, at least. She just needed to get through the next month. At least she had Jayden. He was something else to focus on, something to distract her from her worries. They never talked about work, mostly because he didn't seem to think about Vertex very much when he wasn't in the office. But for Hadley, it felt like all she could think about all day long. She realized she didn't even know if he enjoyed the work he was doing, regardless of his intention to work in an entirely different field eventually. She wondered if she would be honest about her worries if he ever asked.

Hadley needed a distraction today. She had her first major presentation coming up. She was supposed to present the data for a recent social media campaign to the entire marketing communications team and offer a comprehensive analysis on the goals they'd failed to meet and offer suggestions for improvement. She hadn't started yet, which wasn't like her at all. She'd tried a couple of times to start sifting through the data, but every time she did, all of the numbers and graphs and projections started to blur together, and she had to click off.

Today she needed to buckle down, but she started to feel a headache coming on just thinking about the amount of work yet to do. It really wasn't like her. She was a planner. She liked to schedule what tasks she would complete each day leading up to a deadline. But even pulling out a sheet of paper to make a to-do list seemed pointless.

She found herself thinking about hanging out with Jayden instead.

As if on cue, she felt her phone vibrate in her pocket. She slipped it out, surreptitiously, flat on the desk where no one could see, and saw a text from Jayden.

Happy Friday! What are we doing later?

She couldn't help but smile. *Takeout and a movie? Maybe too boring for you, but I need to decompress.*

She had hardly pressed send when he replied. *As long as we get Thai.*

Hadley tucked her phone away again and turned back to her computer. Surely the prospect of a relaxing night would give her the boost she needed to start sorting the data for her presentation. She clicked open the first spreadsheet.

───

Only a few hours later, Hadley and Jayden were sitting on the couch in his living room devouring their pad Thai and watching *The Avengers*. It wasn't exactly the most romantic movie they could've picked, but as they were browsing their streaming options, they had discovered their mutual love of Marvel and decided to go for a classic.

Hadley glanced over at Jayden to see him watching the screen intently and mouthing almost every line. She couldn't stop a small giggle from escaping her lips, and he turned sharply to look at her, eyes wide.

"I could probably quote most of this," said Jayden, a bit sheepish, his cheeks and temples turning just barely pink.

"So could I," Hadley replied. "I'm doing everything I can to hold it in, so I'm not too annoying."

"It's not annoying." Jayden offered her a smile. "It's cute."

Hadley felt her face flush a little bit. She scooped another forkful of pad Thai into her mouth.

It had been so refreshing to walk out the main door of Vertex headquarters with something to look forward to besides dinner and a good night's sleep. Hadley insisted on paying for the Thai takeout to thank Jayden for hosting her. Again. She wasn't sure she was ready to risk him running into her parents at home just yet. So they had been curled on the couch since they arrived, chatting, eating, and watching together, two full days of freedom ahead of them. Even just pushing off her existential fears about her future and her career was draining for Hadley, so on top of the stress of getting her actual work done, she was mentally exhausted. She wanted a true night off, but even here, even with the television on, food in her hands, and Jayden by her side, the thoughts flickered through her head.

Where to go from here? How was she going to finish her presentation? How was she going to finish the internship? What was she going to do with her life if she had to imagine new dreams and goals for herself? She tried to banish her thoughts by focusing on the plan to combat Loki and recover the Tesseract, but even the Avengers' witty banter wasn't helping too much.

Hadley shifted her weight off the couch armrest and leaned into Jayden's side, worry lines creasing her forehead. He, in turn, shifted to curve his body around her and wrapped an arm around her shoulder. He looked down, and she did her best to relax her face. She set down her nearly empty takeout box on the coffee table.

What was Jayden going to think if she told him she had no idea what she was doing with her life anymore? She didn't want to be thinking about this. She wanted to be present in this moment, enjoying the time they were spending together. But she couldn't. Not with all this noise in her head and knots in her stomach. She needed to do something.

All she knew was what had worked last time. Hadley craned her neck up and kissed Jayden again. This time, however, it was more passionate, fervent. It was almost desperate. He responded, throwing his other arm around her waist and pulling her even closer. She put her hands on his chest, started to fumble with the buttons on his shirt. It was working—she was fully focused on Jayden.

But then he pulled her hands away. Hadley was confused. Maybe he wanted to take it off himself? That was fine. Still kissing him, she started to pull up on the hem of her own shirt.

Jayden pulled back.

"Whoa, Hadley, slow down."

Hadley sat up straight, yanking her hands away from him. "What?"

"I just—" He seemed just as flustered as her.

"What?" Hadley said again. Her confusion was starting to be usurped by red hot embarrassment, and she pressed her back into the far corner of the small couch as hard as she could. What did he mean? He didn't want to be with her? Maybe he had realized he didn't actually like her that way. Maybe he was about to reject her right here, and then she would have ruined their entire friendship.

"What's going on? Is everything okay?" he asked, reaching for the remote.

Hadley shook her head vigorously, then, registering his question, switched quickly to nodding. "I'm fine. Don't pause it. It's fine. Keep watching. I should probably go anyways." What had she done? He was disgusted with her. Could he have glimpsed the desperation in her eyes? The need to do anything to distract herself. He must have seen right through her.

"Hadley, wait."

"No, no, I really need to go." Hadley scrambled to her feet, fumbling for her phone in the crack between the couch cushions. She backed toward the kitchen, where her purse was on the counter. She hadn't meant to use him. She really liked him, but she'd gone too far, and she didn't know how to explain it to him. She'd ruined everything.

"Hadley, please, just wait." Jayden got up and started walking toward her, abandoning the remote and the still-playing movie.

"Later," said Hadley. "We can talk later. I'll text you. I just have to go."

She snatched up her bag and practically ran for the door. She didn't even close it behind her. Not wanting to wait for the elevators, she hurried past them to the stairwell. She didn't look to see if Jayden had followed her out. She just got out of there as fast as she could. Her heart rate didn't start to slow until she had driven fifteen blocks away, and then, as the red faded from her cheeks, she started to cry.

14

OCTOBER

Midterms had arrived in full force. Hadley was running on four hours of sleep, a sharp decline from her usual seven or eight. She had perpetually too much to do and not enough time to do it all. Her essays were nothing but half-formed outlines, her exam studying no more than a stack of notes to flip through. She was quickly losing her grasp on her plans for a successful midterm, successful semester, and successful year. At this point, she wasn't quite sure where to begin.

She had tried working alone, isolated in her bedroom or back in her newfound study spot in the math building, purposely spending enough time there so Amy couldn't accuse her of spending too much time in the dorm. But in that space, it was too easy to get distracted by her phone, her email, and the internet, and in her room, it was too easy to get distracted by, well, everything.

Today, she needed to try something new. She was risking a venture into the main floor of the student center with her roommates, hopeful that being with other students in the same midterm crunch as her would motivate her to buckle down.

She texted Bianca and Amy she was on her way as she left class, trying to focus on typing and not tripping as she jogged down the steps and simultaneously tallying each thing she needed to get done today. First and foremost, she needed to crank out a draft of the essay due soonest—and fast. The sooner she had that done, the easier it would be to go back through and revise and put it in her own head that she had something nearly done. Another mind trick to keep herself motivated. Then, she needed to go over at least a third of her notes for her first exam. After that, she needed to prep for her meeting with the counselor from the Career Center, coming up with intelligent-sounding questions to ask and a few avenues to pursue. That was doable. If she really stuck to it, she could get all of those things done and get her to-do list down to a manageable length.

Bianca and Amy were sitting at a table near the cafe, notebooks, loose pieces of paper, cords, and pencils scattered across its surface. The room was crowded, with nearly every table occupied by harried and disheveled students.

Bianca looked up as Hadley approached. "There she is," she said. "Get over here, H. We need your academic confidence to help us get our lives together."

Hadley laughed, though she cringed internally at the mention of her purported academic confidence. She was probably the last thing her roommates needed if they wanted to get their lives together. "I'm here to help." She set down her bag and helped her roommates restack their papers and rearrange their workspaces like she always did.

"You're a miracle worker," said Amy.

"I don't know how you always have your life so put together. I'm actually drowning in work right now," said Bianca, slumping down into her chair.

"So am I," said Hadley, but she was smiling. She didn't quite know how to turn off her reflex to appear forever calm in the face of stress. She wished she could convince Bianca she felt the exact same way.

After setting up her own space, Hadley got to work on her tasks. She fleshed out the outline of her paper, compiled the necessary quotes and evidence she needed, and dual-screened the outline with her blank draft document. This was how she worked best. She started to relax. It really did help to be with her roommates, in the zone, together. She started typing away at her introduction.

The sun had descended just far enough in the sky that it was casting slight shadows across Hadley's carefully arranged workspace, and she'd nearly finished her second cup of coffee of the day, when a familiar voice yanked her from her mind-set of disciplined concentration.

"HD?" Jayden was standing not ten feet away looking at her, his tone tentative, with a similar mix of surprise, wistfulness, and fear splashed across his face as Hadley herself was feeling when she looked up at him. He had a distinct five o'clock shadow, he was carrying a tall stack of papers, and Hadley found herself oddly surprised he was susceptible to midterm stress like everybody else.

Then the panic started to set in. She was looking at him, he was looking at her, and she could feel Bianca and Amy's eyes trained on her, too.

"Hi," she said.

Jayden took a half-step forward, then seemed to think better of it and stopped again.

"Who is this?" asked Bianca, kicking Hadley under the table.

Hadley hardly heard the question, and it seemed Jayden hadn't heard either because neither of them said anything. They just kept looking at each other. Hadley felt her stomach start to churn and her chest tighten, an all-too-familiar feeling that only increased her panic. The moment of silence continued to drag on, and her head began to spin.

"How... How are you doing?" said Jayden finally, taking a full step forward this time. "I didn't know—"

"Fine," said Hadley, looking down at the table.

"I've wanted to talk to you," he continued. "Could we talk?"

"Oh." She flushed. Could she think of nothing better to say? "I-I don't think this is a good time. We're working." She gestured toward her roommates.

"It's okay," said Bianca unhelpfully. "We're fine. We can also—" She looked back and forth between the two of them, confusion evident on her face. Amy was leaning ever so slightly forward in her seat, wide-eyed, watching the exchange. "Amy and I... We can leave?" Bianca looked at Hadley.

"No, no. It's okay," she said to Bianca. "Now's not a good time," she said to Jayden. "I really... There's a lot going on right now. It's not a good time."

"I just want to talk," said Jayden, his face falling even as he spoke. "I wanted to tell you—"

"No!" said Hadley. She stood up out of her chair, flipping her laptop shut. "Seriously, not now." She looked at her roommates, then back at Jayden. All three of them looked confused, expectant, and hurt. "I have to go. I need to focus. I need space." Hadley didn't know what she needed, but her heart rate wasn't slowing down, and she knew she had to get somewhere where she could calm herself down. She was feeling too much like she did over the summer, and she could not—she would not—have a repeat of that. Not today. Not right now. "I have to go," she said again, throwing all of her belongings back into her bag with no regard for the folded pages and uncapped pens.

She started to walk away from the table. Bianca and Amy were glancing over at each other, having a frantic conversation with their eyes. Jayden was staring at her, not moving, his mouth hanging slightly open.

"Sorry," she said, and she was gone, weaving between the tables, between groups of students studying, headed straight for the doors.

Hadley couldn't stop walking. She tried to take a couple of deep breaths as she hurried away from her friends, from Jayden, but she couldn't seem to slow the beating of her heart. She fumbled with her bag, trying to straighten up the mess inside, the jumble of papers, the folded open notebooks, the loose writing utensils, the laptop out of its case. Everything was out of its place. She needed to get it straightened out.

She didn't know where she was going—only that she needed to be as far from the student center as possible—until she looked up and realized she was heading straight for the mental health center. She wanted to stop herself. She wanted to turn around and go back to her dorm, or the library, or anywhere else where she could sit down and try to refocus on her work, but her legs kept moving, and her mind started to piece together that her body already knew where she needed to be right now.

Hadley hardly remembered walking through the lobby. She paused to wait for the elevator, feet tapping impatiently, before pivoting toward the stairs. She took them two at a time, each flight a blur, but somehow she stopped at the right floor. She pushed open the door of the mental health clinic and walked straight toward the hallway that led to Angie's office.

"Excuse me, do you have an appointment?" Hadley turned to see the receptionist, half-standing up out of her chair, waving in her direction to get her attention.

"I have to see Dr. Rowe. I'm here to see Dr. Rowe." She felt flustered. She could feel the heat rising in her cheeks, but she didn't have time to pause. She needed to get into that office, onto that couch.

"Do you have an appointment?" the receptionist repeated. "I can't let you go in without an appointment."

Hadley felt her hands start to get clammy and her heart pound. She needed to see Angie. She couldn't wait and come back another time. "I... You don't understand. I need—"

"Hadley?" Angie was standing in the opening of the hallway at the back of the waiting room. A mug was steaming in her hand. Hadley walked quickly toward her.

"I need to talk to you," she said, breathless. "I need to tell you what happened."

15

AUGUST

The first slide of Hadley's presentation was blank in front of her, taunting her with the white expanse she had yet to fill. Jayden probably hated her. He'd tried calling her a couple of times over the weekend, and he'd sent a couple of texts asking to talk, but she couldn't face him and hadn't replied. She hadn't seen him yet today. He was probably avoiding her now. And who could blame him? She'd been a complete idiot, so wrapped up in herself and her own problems and the fact that she hated this job and didn't know how she would tell her parents or what she would do with her life. How was she supposed to focus on a social media marketing report when everything was crashing down around her?

Who was she going to sit with at lunch? She didn't think she had the strength to face Jayden. Not today. She might just have to skip lunch altogether or grab something from the vending machine. Best-case, she could run in and grab something from the salad bar. In and out, before anyone had a chance to register her presence at all.

And she didn't know how the hell she was going to put together this presentation. "Focus," she muttered to herself.

Katie and the rest of the marketing team must have thought she was utterly incapable. She just hoped she could recover from this and salvage her reputation at Vertex. Or maybe she should just accept marketing wasn't for her. But then again, if this wasn't going to be her career path, what was? This was her only plan. She didn't have a backup. Hadley needed a return offer because at least then she would have a life ahead of her, even if it was one she didn't want. She needed to start working on her presentation.

Hadley could feel herself starting to sweat, despite the blast of the air conditioner. Perspiration was beginning to pool at her temples. She wiped at them with the sleeve of her denim jacket and then took it off, tossing it over the back of her chair. She placed her elbows strategically wide on the desk, hoping more airflow to her underarms would cool her down faster. She didn't know what was going on. Clearly, her body was working against her, too. Absolutely everything that could go wrong was going wrong, and she didn't know how to get things to stop. She was even losing control over her own body.

The fact was she had messed up the only good thing to happen to her this summer and, more than likely, her parents would soon find out some way or another that she wanted to abandon the career path they were so proud of, and then she would have no one. She could picture the barely concealed disappointment on their faces. She hardly kept in touch with her high school friends, and they wouldn't understand anyway. Not to mention no part of her wanted the pity from Bianca and Amy and all her friends at school if they found out she had no idea what she wanted to do with her life and had to basically start from scratch. She knew the back-to-school drill. Everyone would be asking everyone about their summer jobs, and she would either have to tell them everything had gone horribly wrong or lie.

She was stuck between all bad options. It was a lose-lose. Hadley really didn't want to have to deal with any of this. She wanted it all to go away, but this weight on her chest was making it really hard to breathe, and all she could think about was having to avoid Jayden for the rest of the summer and back on campus in the fall, too. The blank presentation slide was staring at her, her cursor flashing in the title box, and she struggled to even catch her breath.

It felt like her whole world—everything she had ever worked for, all the hours she'd put into studying and researching and interviewing—was crumbling in front of her eyes. The debris was piling up on her chest, weighing her down, and she couldn't breathe.

A bead of sweat dripped down her underarm on the inside of her dress. Hadley pressed the fabric into her side to wipe it away, and a small wet stain bloomed through the thin white material.

She didn't have a next move. She always had a next move, but right now, she couldn't even seem to get a single word onto her presentation. She was starting to feel very light-headed, and her breath came in short, fast gasps. She needed to get out of here, out of this stupid flex space, before people started to think something was wrong, even though, of course, everything was wrong.

Hadley got up from her desk and, avoiding eye contact with Dina, stumbled toward the bathroom. There was a group of people clustered around one of the whiteboards, so she kept her head down, hoping she wouldn't catch their attention. She was going to make a complete fool of herself, sweating and gasping like this in front of everyone, but she couldn't stop the flood of anxious thoughts. It felt like nothing could relieve the weight on her chest. If only she could catch her breath.

She pushed open the door and felt the stale air of the windowless bathroom slam into her nose and mouth. She ran straight for the nearest stall. She barely had time to lock the door behind her and pull back her hair before she was vomiting into the toilet bowl.

Once she was fairly certain her entire breakfast had come back out the same way it had come in, she leaned back against the side of the stall, trying to catch her breath. She felt sweaty and clammy and shaky all at once. Her head was spinning, and her stomach was rumbling. This was a disaster. How embarrassing to have thrown up in the middle of a workday. No one could know. She would just have to clean herself up the best she could and get back to her desk, her work, and that blank presentation. She had to finish that presentation.

Hadley flushed the toilet twice and unlocked the stall, making a beeline to the sink to rinse her face and mouth. It wasn't until she finally looked up, face dripping wet, hair and clothes disheveled, that she saw Katie standing three sinks over, looking at her in the mirror with some mixture of concern and disgust on her face.

"Hadley? Are you okay? I heard..." Katie trailed off, unsure.

Hadley's head started to spin even faster than before. She'd been seen, and by Katie no less. Her boss! How could she fix this? She had to fix this. It was going to be hard to cover up, but she couldn't—she wouldn't—let anyone know. The most important thing was getting out of this bathroom, collecting herself, then getting back to her desk and back to work. She just needed to act normal. If only she could manage a deep breath.

"I'm fine, I'm fine," she said, entirely unconvincing, trying to smooth her hair, adjust her dress, and walk toward the door at the same. She couldn't be here right now. She had to get away from Katie. She just needed a minute to herself—a minute to get everything under control.

"Are you sure? It sounded like—"

"I'm fine. I'm good. I think I just ate something bad." Good, that was believable. As Hadley moved to open the door, it was pushed open by an older employee. The woman did a double-take when she saw her standing immediately on the other side of the door, but Hadley pushed past her back into the office flex space. She needed to get out of here.

She glanced toward her desk and, leaning against the wall behind her chair, she saw Jayden. He saw her too. Her head started to spin faster.

"Hadley, there you are. I wanted to—Hey, are you okay?"

Dina looked up from her laptop and stared at Hadley. Jayden started to walk toward her, his question drawing the gazes of more people. It felt as though every eye was on her.

No, this couldn't happen. She needed to be alone! She needed to get everything under control. Not now. Not now! Hadley started to back away, feeling the entire situation, the entire summer, her entire life, slip out of her grasp.

"I'm fine," she said.

Then she collapsed.

16

OCTOBER

"And that's basically everything that happened this summer," said Hadley. "I spent the rest of the day in the hospital while the doctor tried to talk my parents out of their own panic, but they insisted I take some time at home, and I couldn't face going back to work anyways. So that's how my glamorous Vertex internship ended. For the last few weeks of summer, I was at home watching Netflix and convincing my mom to let me come back to school, and I haven't spoken to Jayden at all until just now. I haven't talked to anyone about what happened. Not even my roommates."

Angie handed her a tissue, and when she held it up to her face, Hadley discovered she was crying. "Thank you for sharing that with me, Hadley."

Hadley wiped away her tears as best as she could.

"How are you feeling?" Angie asked. "That was a lot to put out there."

Hadley took a deep breath. "Better than I look, actually. It feels good to say it all."

"I'm glad to hear that. It must be nice not to have to hold it in anymore."

Hadley nodded.

Angie looked down at her notepad for a moment—considering, then set it aside. "What do you need right now, Hadley? What do you think would be most useful for you? We could talk some more about what happened and try to work through some of those feelings, or we could talk about what comes next."

"What do you mean what comes next?"

"I mean strategies for moving forward. Of course, we'll want to spend some more time talking about some of what you went through this summer, but I'd like to hear what you think would best serve you right now."

"All I want is to move forward," said Hadley. And it was true. That was all she had wanted ever since it happened, but apparently, she'd made no progress at all, and what she'd just felt, caught between Jayden and her roommates in the student center, was precariously close to what she'd felt in the days leading up to her panic attack. "I just feel overwhelmed, and I don't know how to get out of my own head."

"I'd like to try something different today," said Angie. "I know you like plans, and you like to be organized, and while there's no real way to say exactly when and how you'll be able to work through all of this, we can set some goals and come up with strategies to reach them. We can focus on solutions for the situation you're in right now. How does that sound?"

Angie handed Hadley a blank notepad and had her come up with a list of things she wanted to happen in the wake of her experience over the summer. Hadley felt some power sitting in this room with a notepad of her own, and it made her want to be fully honest with Angie and with herself. She wrote that she wanted to refocus on school, figure out where to go next in terms of her career, reconnect with her roommates, and be able to face Jayden.

"Let's take this step by step," said Angie. "What is stopping you from focusing on school?"

"I think bottling up what happened over the summer. My panic attack is part of it. I'm mostly just feeling like I have too much on my mind, so I don't even know where to start fixing things."

"That's understandable. So what about right now? Let's talk about what you have on your plate."

Hadley rattled off her list of midterms, assignments, and extracurricular responsibilities she had coming up in the next week or so, as well as her various degrees of partial completion, or noncompletion, of each. Angie helped her list out everything she needed to do to complete each assignment, as well as the time and energy it would take. Realizing the near impossibility of meeting all of her deadlines, Hadley started to get flustered again. She shifted in her seat and took a couple of deep breaths.

"It's okay, Hadley," said Angie. "We can figure this out. You have a lot on your mind, so it's good that you're here right now looking for help, and I'm not the only person who can give it to you. Your midterms may be hard to move, but I can certainly help you reach out to your adviser and your professors to request extensions on the papers."

Together, they drafted an email to send to Hadley's professors with Angie's backing. Then, they prioritized Hadley's extracurricular commitments to find the places she valued the most and the places where she could take a step back for the time being.

"We have a plan now for the next few weeks, but this kind of planning is something we can revisit again if you ever want to," said Angie. "Moving on to your job concerns, what is most important to you in thinking about what you want to do next?"

"I feel like I focus the best when I have a destination, so I've been looking for an answer about what I'm going to pursue so I can start working toward it. I think not having that destination is part of what's making me so stressed, too."

"I understand that. But it sounds to me like you're more concerned with finding a new destination than with finding the right destination."

Hadley considered her answer carefully. "I guess I'm just nervous about what it means for me not to know what I want to do after graduation."

"Lots of people still don't know exactly what they want to do. More than you think, probably. And plenty more decide to switch career paths as you did, but many don't figure that out until much farther along." Angie looked at Hadley, her head cocked just slightly to one side. "You know, if the only thing you learned from your internship was that you don't want to be in marketing, that still sounds to me like it was worth your while. Better to figure that out now, don't you think?"

"I guess," said Hadley. "But it would still have been nicer if I got it right in the first place. I put so much time into just getting to Vertex, and I hated it. I completely misjudged myself and what I wanted."

"Which is why I think you shouldn't rush into the next thing. You have time. And you have resources. Instead of your goal being finding a career path, maybe your goal should just be to spend some time exploring your options."

Hadley told Angie about her appointment at the Career Center. In turn, Angie encouraged her to spend just ten or so minutes a day researching companies she was potentially interested in and reaching out to alumni to speak with them about their careers. "Perhaps we can spend some more time on this next week once you speak to the career counselor," she said. "But I'd really like to talk about Bianca, Amy, and Jayden today."

Hadley took another deep breath, letting herself sink back into her seat. After a momentary pause, she swung her legs up and laid back on the chaise longue. "Where to begin?"

"Let's start with your roommates," said Angie. "What do you think has stopped you from talking to them about your time at Vertex?"

"A lot of things," Hadley admitted. "I feel like they have this image of me. I'm the mature one. I'm the organized one. I'm the one who's always supposed to know exactly what I'm doing at all times. I just didn't want them to stop thinking of me that way. Actually…" She paused. "It's not even that. I would be fine if they didn't think of me that way, but it's more the breaking of that image I'm not too excited about."

"Do you think they wouldn't react well?"

"I don't know," Hadley admitted. "That's kind of the problem. I don't know how they would react, and that makes me nervous."

"They might surprise you," said Angie. "But even if they don't, you might get something out of it just from getting it off your chest."

"That is how I felt today, talking to you," said Hadley. "I think that's why I came here. Part of me knew that's what I needed. I wasn't planning to. I wasn't thinking. I just started walking."

"I think the most important thing is you do what you think will be the best for you and your own mental wellbeing. It seems to me like that means talking to them if your goal is to reconnect. But talking doesn't have to mean sharing everything if you don't want it to."

Hadley would have to think about it. She knew Bianca and Amy would have questions for her when she got back to the room. She shuddered to think about what words and expressions had been exchanged when she left them at the table with Jayden.

Jayden. Angie wanted to talk about him next.

"How do you feel about that situation? It seems like a lot was still unsaid when you left Vertex."

Hadley could feel her cheeks go pink. "I don't know what to do about him. I'm the type of person, when I wake up after a night of drinking and I've texted someone I shouldn't have texted, I just delete the whole thread. I don't want to read it. I don't want to know what I've done. That's kind of how I feel about Jayden right now."

Hadley could tell Angie was trying not to laugh at her example. "Well, do you think that's fair to him? You don't know what he might want to say to you. It's similar to your roommates. You don't know how they'll react."

Hadley sighed. "I guess I'm kind of embarrassed. I feel horrible about what happened. I really liked him—like him, but I was going after him for all the wrong reasons. He was the only thing that could distract me from my stress, but it wasn't fair to use him like that. I don't know how to tell him all that, though."

"I think you did a pretty good job right there," said Angie, smiling.

By the time their hour was up, Hadley was feeling strong. Not quite confident, not quite *good*, but strong.

Finally, she had some options, if not quite a plan. And, surprisingly, she was okay not knowing exactly what came next.

17

OCTOBER

When Hadley got back from Angie's office, Bianca and Amy were sitting on the common room couch studying, much in the same positions she had left them in at the student center. Side by side, they looked serene—the kind of calm Hadley needed right now—surrounded by a smattering of study materials and snacks off the snack shelf. They looked up as she walked in. Hadley braced herself.

"There you are," said Bianca. She put down her pencil and set her notebook off to one side.

"Are you okay?" Amy asked. "We tried calling you, but we figured you would end up back here at some point."

"I went to see my therapist," said Hadley.

"Your therapist? What therapist?" Bianca asked, looking over at Amy to gauge whether she was the only one out of the loop.

"I've been seeing one of the counselors on campus this semester. It's a long story, but I'd like to tell it." She set down her bag and, though her roommates started to clear a spot on the couch, curled up in the armchair opposite them. "First, I need to tell you guys about my summer internship."

The girls still looked confused, but after exchanging a glance, they seemed to decide to go with it. "The almighty Vertex," said Bianca. "What about it?"

"About time," said Amy. "You haven't told me a thing about your summer."

"I'm not exactly sure where to start," said Hadley, but start she did, for the second time that day. It wasn't quite as thorough as the account she gave Angie, but she kept the most salient parts in. She talked about the worries she'd had—and suppressed—even from her very first days at Vertex and how her distaste for her internship had only grown. She talked about how she didn't want to admit to herself she was on the wrong path and how she'd been hoping to set herself straight this semester. She told them about her panic attack, though she glossed over some of the gritty details about the buildup and the way she'd felt that day and exactly how it all went down. She mentioned the hospital visit, though she assured them it was out of an abundance of caution. And she talked about how overwhelmed she felt, between school, planning for the future, and trying to carry all of the unspoken emotions. "I feel like I've been on edge this whole semester. Worried it's going to happen again, I guess."

Amy got up and squeezed in next to Hadley on the armchair, wrapping an arm around her.

"And what about that guy from earlier? Is he—" Bianca stopped, shooting Amy a look. Hadley wondered what had happened after she fled the student center, whether Jayden and her roommates had exchanged any words, and what they had gleaned from the whole event. But they didn't bring it up, and she didn't ask.

"I met him there, at Vertex. He worked there too. We—" She paused, not sure exactly how to define their relationship or how she'd misused it. "We hung out a lot. But I hid all my anxieties from him, too. And I was embarrassed when my panic attack happened and everything. I haven't talked to him since that day. Until today, I guess."

"Wow," said Amy. "I'm sorry all that happened." She squeezed Hadley's shoulder.

"Thanks for telling us," said Bianca.

There was a moment of quiet.

"So what are you going to do now?" Amy asked, tentative.

"I don't really know." Hadley wasn't quite sure exactly what Amy was referring to, but either way, she figured she didn't know.

"What are you going to do about Vertex? That was your dream company. Are you going to try to go back, maybe in a different department? I guess it depends on what they said about—about what happened," said Bianca.

Hadley tried not to let the sting of the words show on her face. Bianca meant well, she reminded herself. Hadley hadn't described every little thing that happened, so how could she expect Bianca to know what she didn't want to hear.

"I don't think I want to go back. I kind of have to start from scratch in terms of figuring out what's next and what I actually want to do." Hadley caught herself distractedly picking at the upholstery of the armchair and pulled her fingers away.

"I'm sorry," said Amy. "That sucks. We're here for you, though. I'm glad you told us."

This wasn't exactly what Hadley was hoping for either. She wasn't looking for pity. In fact, she really didn't want it. She knew they were trying to be nice, so she would just have to grit her teeth and get through the awkwardness. She'd sprung all this on them, really. No friends were perfect, but she was lucky Bianca and Amy were just about as close to perfect as they could get.

"Thanks," said Hadley. "I think everything just kind of built up today. I have so much work to do, and the stress got to me."

"You don't have to tell me." Bianca threw her feet up onto the couch and laid back. "I have five million things to do and not nearly enough time to do them."

"Me too," said Amy. "We can do some roommate study sessions to really buckle down and knock some stuff out."

"I think there's lots of takeout in our future," said Bianca.

"That's exactly what I need," said Hadley. She was grateful, really, for her friends. Telling them what had been going on had actually gone pretty well—much better than she had feared. She could tell that, though they were compassionate, they couldn't quite understand where she was coming from. She supposed after two years of hyping up her plans for the future and her dreams of working at a company like Vertex, she couldn't blame them for not immediately understanding her turnaround, two months after they thought she success-fully completed a summer internship there.

They were kind, and they cared about her, but they didn't fully understand. And there was only one person who would.

18

OCTOBER

Hadley took deep breaths to calm her nerves as she exited the Career Center and walked toward the campus Starbucks. She'd just left a meeting with one of the career counselors, which had been surprisingly helpful, providing her with a number of resources to aid in her exploration as well as continued reinforcement that she was not alone in her uncertainty. But all of that flew from her mind as soon as she stepped out of the building.

She had asked Jayden to meet her for a coffee to talk. She hadn't said much more than that in the text message, and he had written back almost immediately to say yes. Hadley truly had no idea what he was going to say to her or, for that matter, what she was going to say to him. She didn't know if she should explain herself, apologize, or just let him do the talking and let herself have the talking-to she deserved after the way she'd acted. She was embarrassed. She could already feel herself start to sweat, and her face start to get warm, but she knew she couldn't start working on herself until she had this situation sorted out. In order to stick to the plans she'd made with Angie, she couldn't be wasting energy perpetually trying to avoid Jayden.

He was already there, of course, when she walked into the Starbucks, sitting at a table with two drinks in front of him—a still presence amongst the bustle of the coffee shop, streaked with the sunlight that floated in through the wide front windows. He looked just the same as he had that summer—less disheveled than when she'd last seen him, leaning back into his seat to make himself comfortable, but she could see his nerves in the way he tapped his foot on the floor. He looked up and started to stand when he saw her approach, then flushed and sat back down. Hadley looked at the two cups on the table.

"I didn't want to have to fight with you to let me pay," he explained without her having to say a word, his cheeks still pink. "But I realize I probably should've let you pick your own drink. I just got a latte like you used to get at work." He scratched his head absentmindedly and slid one of the coffees over to her.

"Thanks," said Hadley, giving him a small smile as she sat down across from him. She couldn't help the slight glow she felt in her chest at the idea he had remembered her coffee order, but she tried not to get her hopes up. He was acting almost normal. Maybe he was going to be nice and let her down easy. Come to think of it, she couldn't really imagine Jayden being mean at all, though this was different than any conversation they'd had before. The stakes felt higher.

"How are you?" she asked because she didn't know what else to say.

"I'm okay. Midterms. You know." He didn't go on, and they both took a long sip of their coffees and avoided eye contact with each other. Around them, the sea of cafe chatter went on, but their bubble, silent in the midst of it all, grew.

"I'm sorry," they said at the same time, breaking the prolonged pause. Then they both stared at each other, wide-eyed, a bit confused, but also finding it a little funny.

"You can go first," said Hadley, quickly taking a gulp of her drink.

"I guess I wanted to apologize," Jayden began. "I mean, I did want to apologize for how we left things. I felt horrible after that day at my place when you left, and I wanted to come to your desk to talk to you about it in person, but then—you know. And I've felt so bad about it ever since. I just hoped I wasn't part of the reason it happened, but I feel like I had to be, if that isn't too self-centered of me. When you didn't answer my texts and calls after you left work, I figured you probably didn't want to talk to me, but I saw you in the student center the other day, and I had to say something."

"You shouldn't feel bad at all!" Hadley said, alarmed at the realization he thought her panic attack was somehow his fault. Of course, her stress about their relationship had been on her mind, but that was her own doing. "I wanted to apologize to you for how I acted when we were hanging out at your apartment. I—" She covered her face with her hand and took a deep breath. "I was in such a bad place at work and, this is going to sound bad, but I think I was looking for anything to distract me. And you didn't deserve that. Because I really liked—like—you and I went about it all the wrong way. Honestly, I got in my own head, and I didn't want you to feel obligated to reach out to me, so I thought it was better just to leave everything alone once I left Vertex."

Hadley watched as something like relief spread across Jayden's face. She wondered if the same look was crossing her own.

"So you do like me?" he said.

Hadley felt a rush spread through her body. "That's what you got from what I just said?"

"That's the important part. The rest—what happened over the summer, how we left things—if you're willing to let it go, then I've already forgotten it." He reached across the table and grabbed her hand. "The important thing is you're not in that bad place anymore."

"Don't get your hopes up," said Hadley. "I may not be in a bad place, but I'm still a mess. I have nothing figured out." She scanned his face, but he didn't flinch.

"Nothing figured out is just the way I like it." He squeezed her hand. "Do you want to talk about any of it?"

Hadley thought about it. "Yes," she said, and she found she was telling the truth. "But not right now."

"Okay," said Jayden. "Then what do you want to do right now?"

"No idea," she said. "And I'm open to anything." She paused. "As long as there's food involved."

"A woman after my own heart," he said. "Let's get out of here."

ACKNOWLEDGMENTS

I was lucky enough to have thousands of conversations, suggestions, and words of support from dozens of people during the process of writing this book, without which I would never have made it this far. For all this and more, I would like to thank my parents, Liam Lavery and Yazmin Mehdi, who are my most infallible support system. I must thank my brother, Declan Lavery, for the inspired suggestions, even though I didn't end up including a car chase or fight scene. Thank you to my grandparents, Bill and Barb Lavery, for preordering copies for all their friends, and to my *abuelita*, Maria Mehdi, for being my motivation.

Special thanks to Eric Koester for the opportunity, to the entire Creator Institute and New Degree Press team, and especially to my editors Camryn Privette and Karina Agbisit, for doing everything in their power to keep me on track and for helping drag me across the finish line.

Thank you to my lovely best friends Sydney Horn and Sophie Lamb for being candid with me about their own experiences with anxiety and to my other best friends Karina Ascunce, Katrina Hon, and Charlotte Ruhl for cheering me on. To my beautiful cousin, Flora Mehdi, for being only herself every single day and being an example for me to do the same. And to Claire Messud for making me a better writer and for being a light in my world.

I could not have gotten to publication without the support for my presale campaign. For that reason, my most fervent appreciation goes to Liesl Lavery, Yusuf and Stephanie Mehdi, my SOI girls Sahar Mohammadzadeh and Isabella Rhyu, Emory Sabatini, Alicia Vernell Rivera, Jennifer Bernardez, Tembi Karagianes, Lauren Lee, Ben Sikora, Adolphus Adams, Leticia Lopez, Alice Shobe and Eric Svaren, Mollie Ames, Lauren Wattendorf, Grace Handler, Robin Whipple, Nancy Salwen, Siva Sankrithi, Lily Hansen, Menelik Epee-Bounya, Thomas Thongmee, Paula Hoff Zweig, Jennifer Yeung, Kate Laird, Eily Raman, Henry Kendrick, Juan Castaneda, Julianne Johnson, Hallie Hohner, Patricia Corrigan, Sheila G., Gina Lockman, Laura Fentonmiller, and Jennifer Wilson.

Thank you, thank you, thank you.

Made in the USA
Middletown, DE
10 May 2021